Praise for Tandy

"Tandy demonstrated tremendous strength, compassion and unconditional love as the primary caregiver for both of her parents. Providing 24/7 care for both parents simultaneously requires patience, courage and a strong support system. The quality care Tandy's parents received from her and her family extended their lives by several years."

~ Dr. Edouard Mouaikel, MD

"Tandy Elisala is an inspiration and a shining example of how the power of the mind affects healing. As one of Tandy's treating physicians through her last cancer diagnosis, I witnessed her incredible strength and positive attitude. With all of Tandy's life responsibilities during this time, her positive attitude never wavered. I never want to go through what Tandy went through, but if I did, I would look to her as a model for getting through life's challenges."

~ Dr. Todd C. Hobgood, MD

Care Giving Quotes

"In most cases they are unnoticed, because they are the hidden heroes."

~ Elizabeth Dole, on caregivers to wounded warriors

"There are only four kinds of people in the world – those who have been caregivers, those who are caregivers, those who will be caregivers, and those who will need caregivers."

~ Rosalynn Carter

"I think that a caregiver has to ultimately be the advocate for the person with the illness and that means being their ears. I think it's fair enough for the caregiver to be there with the pencil and the paper and asking the questions because when you're the one with the illness, it's so overwhelming sometimes that you don't hear what's being said to you."

~ Meredith Vieira

"Communication has been vital. My advice to every family going through this is to talk honestly with each other."

~ Amy Grant

"When you are a caregiver, you have to think of yourself as the (chief executive) of a very small nursing home."

~ The Wall Street Journal

*More than **65 million people**, 29% of the U.S. population, provide care for a chronically ill, disabled or aged family member or friend during any given year and spend an average of 20 hours per week providing care for their loved one.*

Caregiving in the United States;

National Alliance for Caregiving in collaboration with AARP; November 2009

"Care giving is one of the most gut wrenching, heart breaking journeys you will take but when all is said and done you will never regret one minute of it."

~ Amanda Kaye-Lani Elisala, 24, on caring for her grandparents

Healing
Through the
Chaos:
PRACTICAL CARE GIVING

Tandy Elisala, MA, CPSC, ACH, CHt, TFT-Alg

Edited by:
Tracey Michelle Theisen, MBA, CLC, CPSC

Published by Lightning Source, a subsidiary of
Ingram Press Publishers

available through Ingram Press, and available for
order through Ingram Press Catalogues

This book is a work of non-fiction. Names, conversations, places and incidents have been reconstructed to the best of the author's ability.

Printed in the United States of America

First Printing: November 2013

www.tandyelisala.com

Self Help/Memoir

ISBN: 978-1-62747-031-5

Ebook ISBN: 978-1-62747-032-2

LCN

Table of Contents

Acknowledgments

There are so many who contributed to our family's well being during this difficult time. First and foremost, I thank God for carrying me through my darkest hours and giving me the courage, strength, wisdom, and patience through this journey. When I needed to make difficult decisions and be the head of the family, You gave me courage and strength. When I needed insight or trust, You gave me wisdom and patience. This book is a mere snapshot of the many miracles You've given me and my family, and even now I continue to see the many blessings that have unfolded from that fateful call. Additionally, You also carried me by giving me the most wonderful people in my life, for as Scripture tells us, "Where two or three are gathered, there I am."

While I'm grateful for every person in my life, I'd be remiss not acknowledging a few who helped me along my journey. To my family for their love, support and encouragement, I love you all. Amanda, my daughter, my rock, you are my angel and partner and I am eternally grateful for you. You selflessly put your life on hold to share care giving responsibilities for your grandparents and you did so with unwavering strength and love. You are a wise old soul filled with respect, compassion and love for family; not all 20-year-olds would sacrifice so much to support a family at such a young age. My love for you transcends all words. Sarah, my youngest daughter, and Steven, my son, for being there when it counted, supporting our family in countless ways, and having the strength, love and patience to adapt to our new household, schedule, moving parts and moving in general! The four of us make an awesome team. I love you all to infinity and beyond. Felicity, my sister, I am so thankful to have you with me in this life. You are a beautiful, intelligent, sensitive, loyal, and devoted sister, daughter, aunt, cousin, teacher, friend and sounding board. I love you, Sis! Uncle Riley, I am so grateful for your love, support, guidance, respite, heavy lifting, and time. Aunt Tandy and Michael, thank you for your visits, heavy lifting, prayers and support. Aunt Mary Ellen, thank you for your prayers, cards, messages, tips, tools, encouragement and love. Thank you for sharing many family stories. I am so thankful that we have grown close and share a mutual love of family history and legacy. You are my Great Aunt in more ways than one. Thank you. A thousand times thank you.

Big thanks go out to my very dear friends; there are too many to list here but I must acknowledge a few. Linda and John, Rose and Brian, Tanna, Mark, and Bess for inspiring, encouraging, loving, and supporting my family and me. You were there for us in countless and various ways, and I am honored to have you in our lives. I am incredibly thankful for Tarra; my spiritual mentor, guide, coach and friend. I wouldn't have made it through this time in my life with as much peace without you. There are countless moments you gave of your talents and time; loving me through it all. Thank you for being you. (P.S. Our fortune cookie memory is forever imprinted in my heart and mind.) To: Nina, Anna, Stacey, Anthony, Sandy, Berlin, Oscar, Terry, John, Clare, Leland, Vince, Laura, Kim, Emily, Tom, Andi, Virginia, Jim C, Nancy, Amanda Z and Mary for your ideas, feedback, cards, calls, meals, physical labor, love, prayers, and support. To my Arizona Job's Daughters family, thank you for your understanding, friendship, support, and love.

To Tracey, what can I say? You came into my life and we quickly became great friends. We both shared our care giving experiences and this is what really connected us. After writing this book and going through second round edits, you graciously volunteered your time, talents, wisdom and vast editing experience to help my book... my story... be the best it can be. Your care giving experience allowed you to see beyond words on a page and helped me heal and feel the story from your eyes. I believe, in many ways, your contributions and many, many hours helping me edit this book helped you heal through your care giving chaos. This book wouldn't be the same without your time, talents, creativity and hard work. I truly, truly appreciate your editing. I know it was a big job; one you enthusiastically took on because of your passion for family care giving. It is because of your tireless editing work, I wanted to honor and recognize you as my book Editor with your name on the cover. I believe everyone comes into our life for a reason. I thank you from the bottom of my heart for everything you did with this massive undertaking. I am excited to see what the future holds for us.

To my canines and felines: thank you for saving us in more ways than one. Your unconditional love, pants, paws, meows, smiles, tail-waggings, and kisses helped get me through my darkest hours. I'm not sure who rescued whom.

We experience different Angels in life, those that are human and those whose presence are felt. Tim, thank you for being our human Angel. You are a stranger turned into a family friend. You saved my dad's life that horrific day by risking yours and you are the reason we had more precious time my dad. I am blessed to know you and your lovely wife, Becky. To the woman who was with my dad in the car that day and helped steer his car to the median rather than into a burning semi, we are all convinced you were my dad's Guardian Angel. I thank every medical professional caring for my parents and having their best interests at heart. No acknowledgement would be complete without thanking the numerous emergency medical staff, fireman, police, doctors, and nurses. This book is dedicated to all of you everywhere. To AmeriCare hospice and palliative care: I have the utmost respect for your organization. Your staff's compassion, professionalism, reassurance, sensitivity, love, passion and care shown to my dad his last days and moments of life provided genuine comfort and peace.

Most of all, thank you **Mom and Dad** for giving me life and raising me to be the person I am today. I wouldn't trade a moment of the time we had together. I love you to infinity and beyond.

.

Foreword by Tracey Michelle Theisen

I was first introduced to Tandy by a mutual friend and was immediately struck by her optimism, grace and kindness. She lights up a room radiating peace, compassion, strength and sincerity; or in one word, authenticity. It was not surprising then that at another encounter I learned she had also been a caregiver. Care giving has a way of gentling the soul, and in Tandy's case it no doubt shined an already bright diamond.

We ended up talking for hours that day about our experiences and discovered incredible similarities in our paths; primarily, that we were both in the height of successful careers when our lives were instantly turned upside down when a relative became ill, sending each into unexpected roles as caregivers. We laughed together and cried together, but mostly expressed gratitude for the amazing, though unintended, curves life threw at us.

Almost in unison, some our first comments to each other were referencing how we thought we were prepared to handle this type of situation but in fact we were very wrong. In my case I ended up being caregiver for my grandparents and endured years of extensive sub acute and chronic home health care giving and medical management; ranging from general aging and limited mobility to stroke rehabilitation to multiple heart surgeries and cancer diagnoses and treatments to wound care and colostomy care, just to name a few. All while still maintaining my full-time career and dealing with the stresses and worries of my father fighting his own battle with cancer half way across the country. Given success in my professional career I thought I could handle any situation, and yet I was utterly unprepared for the exhausting learning curve and the unfathomable time requirements necessary of being an efficient and effective caregiver. Though the help of friends, amazing physicians and medical personnel, and the grace of God I made it through, and I'm proud of what I've learned, done and accomplished. By the end of my journey, my grandfather, father and aunt all passed within months of each other. While being a caregiver is difficult, trying, exhausting, and overwhelming at times, the growth and blessings that emerge are priceless. I feel blessed for having the experience and wear the caregiver badge with pride.

Tandy's story? Well you are about to read Tandy's story. Hers is a truly remarkable journey of survival, dedication, healing through some of the most intense events life could ever throw at one family. It is a remarkable story so compelling it had to be told, for many reasons. First, to reaffirm that even with diverse and unique family backgrounds and situations, the commonalities caregivers experience far outweigh the differences and there is much we can learn from each other in our new roles. Secondly, despite feeling the contrary at times, to let you know that you are not alone in your journey. Third, to offer hope and encouragement that you will indeed come through the tough times, and will be even better for the experience. And finally, for those who are not caregivers but know a caregiver, we hope Tandy's story will give you a glimpse into the everyday life of a caregiver, because often it is the non-caregiver friend, relative, or co-worker who unknowingly is a caregiver to a caregiver.

Tracey Michelle Theisen, MBA, CLC, CPSC

Introduction
What is *Healing through the Chaos*?

A s parents age, children consider the possibility they will become responsible for their parents' care in one way or another. The increase in the life expectancy of the average individual means the situation of caring for an aging parent will become a concern for a growing number of people. Even the most serious considerations of such a responsibility pale in comparison to the actual realities and responsibilities involved in care giving.

My father's car accident and an unexpected illness with my already disabled mother thrust me into the role of caregiver with little warning. My role as a daughter changed dramatically. A strong believer in education, I quickly turned to others for advice and support. I was surprised and dismayed by the lack of depth and insight in available books on the subject. I realized how much I had learned about the role of caregiver and how I had changed and adapted with the role. Most importantly, I realized I had much to share with others facing this challenge—things missing in current publications.

Compassion, healing, peace, and love - these are what we yearn to provide for our loved ones. Yet, when circumstances require us to become caretakers, we often find ourselves overwhelmed, afraid, and awash with feelings of hopelessness. This book is my personal story as I address the challenges of taking on the full time care of both of my parents simultaneously within a short period of time. It covers the full spectrum of trials and tribulations from the surprising shock of my father's devastating accident to learning of my mother's cancer diagnosis to preparing for each of my parents' death, to where I am today; content and driven by my deep desire to help others face and overcome similar challenges.

I want you to know you are not alone. You have the strength to get through any situation and you WILL overcome every experience stronger for it. This book is for every family and individual going through a care-giving and for his or her respective support systems.

Whether it is a tragedy such as a devastating diagnosis or illness or a disabling injury, your life can change in the blink of an eye. Part resource/self help and part memoir, this book takes an inside look into my unexpected journey from corporate executive and entrepreneur to caregiver while raising my children as a single mother and simultaneously going through a third and final bout with cancer. This book is different because it incorporates my personal care giving story, key lessons learned through each stage up to and including death, and provides a transformational family action guide for today's caregiver, tomorrow's caregiver, and those who may need care. Everyone needs a plan TODAY should the unthinkable happen tomorrow. By preparing now and helping loved ones prepare for the unexpected, you demonstrate your unconditional love and gain peace of mind.

This book helps navigate the often confusing, lonely, and exhausting care giving role. I help you through practical matters, key decisions and the myriad of heart-wrenching emotions. I incorporate humor, gratitude, and compassion, and I hope it inspires you to do the same in your life. It provides healing strategies, self-care tips, legacy-building activities, and ways to keep family safe and protected.

Using a practical and personal approach, each chapter guides you through my story, touching on the major care giving obstacles and milestones. Each chapter includes key lessons learned through each stage as I experienced it. With the benefit of both experience and hindsight, the last section of each chapter includes a powerful family action guide to benefit current and future caregivers. You will find that many of the transformational take action items can enhance everyday life.

May this book be a resource for you and your family for years to come. This book promises to help turn chaos into order, hopelessness into hope, helplessness into inspiration, and anger into peace.

Overview

If you have never been a caregiver, chances are you will become one. One in three people in the United States are or will become caregivers in their lifetime.

Ask yourself which of these questions of care giving best identifies your situation?

1. Have you been a caregiver and are reading this thinking, "I wish I had this book when I was caring for my <fill in the blank>"?
2. Were you a caregiver and wonder if it's possible you will give care again?
3. Are you a caregiver today?
4. Do you anticipate or know you will eventually be a caregiver?
5. Will YOU need care someday?
6. Are you breathing?

If you answered YES to any of these questions, then this book is for you.

OK, the question about breathing may seem a silly one. Yet, the American Association of Retired People (AARP) reports that 75 million of us provide care today and the value of unpaid family care giving services will likely continue to be the largest source of long-term care in the U.S. By the year 2030, the aging population 65+ will have more than doubled from 2000[1].

Before we talk about caregiving, let's define the term, *Caregiver*. A caregiver is someone who provides periodic, part-time or full-time care for someone who is ill, disabled or otherwise needs help. Care giving responsibilities can occur suddenly or be anticipated. Caregivers perform a variety of tasks from assisting with daily living activities (such as bathing, dressing, giving medications, taking to doctor's appointments) and/or part-time or full-time 24-hour care.

---

[1] *American Association of Retired People (AARP)*

Many of us take our health and independence for granted. We trust that when we get up each day, our life will be much like it was yesterday, but when an illness or tragedy occurs, your beliefs and assumptions about life are challenged and your faith can be shaken. Sometimes, tragedy, such as a devastating cancer diagnosis or a horrific accident happens and we shake our heads in disbelief and wonder why—Why us? Why me? How could God allow these things to happen? I don't have time for this! I believe everything happens for a reason. We may not understand it or like it, or even agree with it, yet in due time, the situation unfolds and we have the 'ah-ha' moment of clarity.

When tragedy strikes, are you ready…really ready? There are so many thoughts and feelings that run through one's head when something like this happens. It is difficult to describe the vast range of emotions a caregiver might feel every single day, multiple times daily and sometimes hourly. To get a glimpse of my life then, imagine feeling compassionate and then impatient, loving and then angry, productive and then paralyzed, supported and then all alone, calm and then frustrated, hopeful and then sad, beyond stressed and then at peace. Yes, these are a wide range of conflicting emotions that can go round and round in your head.

Have you ever felt?

- Numb? Speechless?
- Tired? Not just tired, but bone tired?
- Sad or depressed?
- Like you are constantly holding your breath?
- Ill prepared to navigate through the myriad of hospitals, doctors, surgeries, case managers, insurance companies?
- Unable to concentrate?
- Unable to put one foot in front of the other?
- Angry you are in this situation?
- Like nobody can possibly help or understand what you are going through?
- All alone?

- Unsure if you are making the right care decisions for loved ones or yourself?
- The weight of the world is on your shoulders?
- You have so much to do you feel paralyzed to do anything?
- So hopeless that you give up even trying to put goals or lists together because you just know you won't get to any of it anyway so why bother?
- Frustrated because you forgot what you went to the next room for; or perhaps realized it's been all day and you haven't gone to the restroom or eaten anything?
- Uncertain whether you are helping or hurting yourself or your loved one?
- Stressed knowing where to find information needed to help?
- Lost in a sea of information from medical professionals who seem like they are speaking a foreign language?
- Have you ever thought these feelings would never end?

I've been there. I've felt it all. I consider myself a pretty self-motivated, independent, and ambitious person. I am a change agent. I get things done. I lead, inspire, speak, motivate, coach, and help others. Others look to me for the answers. Yet imagine my dismay when I became completely lost in this situation. I felt depressed, hopeless, helpless, paralyzed, unmotivated, and wanted to crawl in bed and stay there. This was completely new territory for me. I'm here to tell you, *I got through it* and YOU will get through this and any other life challenges. I promise you will come through the other side of this experience a stronger, wiser, and more peaceful person. Walk with me through my experience and stories of compassion, gratitude, healing, strength and love, and in the process, I think you will learn, grow and be inspired.

My mission with *Healing Through the Chaos* is to help you navigate through the care giving role, whether expected or unexpected. By sharing proven and specific strategies from personal planning, evaluating care needs and options, keeping loved ones safe, to advocate roles, responsibilities and strategies, family activities, to self care tips and honing and evoking your family legacy and everything in between, this book provides a comprehensive life line to everything you need to know about care giving and, in the process, how not to be a burden to your family should you need care one day.

Specifically, you will learn:

1. How to avoid the mistakes I made. You will learn key lessons from someone who has been there.
2. How to take charge of a loved one's care.
3. Things your insurance company won't tell you.
4. Shortcuts for developing a family action guide.
5. Practical family strategies for dealing with the complex and emotional roller coaster ride of the sick or injured. Learn how this can manifest behavior changes and get valuable strategies to manage changing dynamics.
6. How to keep loved ones safe physically, emotionally, mentally and financially.
7. Ways to effectively balance independence and safety.
8. Effective ways to overcome problems inherent through each stage of care giving.
9. How to cope with ongoing challenges of providing care; including your daily life responsibilities.
10. Ways to strengthen both your mind and body and that of your loved one (s).
11. Expert tips on the role gratitude, humor and compassion play in giving care and how to ignite more in your everyday life.
12. How to take care of yourself so you can effectively take care of others.
13. Steps to evaluate short and long term care options. This is one of the most important decisions you will make.
14. Effective ways to build a family legacy. Learn how to draw out special stories, events, feelings, hopes, and dreams.
15. How to NOT be a burden on your family through personal preparation.

16. Why you and your loved ones must have your legal, medical and household affairs in order.
17. Specific strategies to improve communications with medical providers saving time, frustration, money and sanity.
18. **You are not alone, and everything you are experiencing is okay. You WILL get through this.**

As a result, you will have:

1. Immediately beneficial tools for navigating the myriad of feelings, thoughts and decisions associated with care giving.
2. Invaluable consolidated practical resources for every care giving stage.
3. Insider personal household tips for you and your entire family.
3. A family action guide to prepare for your tomorrows.

As a result, you will BE....

at PEACE.

Who Is Who?

There were a lot of simultaneous things happening throughout my journey, and as I wrote this book, it became apparent that the 'cast of characters' could become confusing. Here is a brief introduction, including some of their ages at the onset of this journey.

1. William (Bill) Stevens: My father
2. Carolyn K Stevens: My mother
3. Amanda Elisala: My oldest daughter, 19 and living at home.
4. Sarah Elisala: My daughter, 16 and living at home.
5. Steven Elisala: My son, 14 and living at home.
6. Berlin: Sarah's friend, 16 and lived with us for 11 months.
7. Felicity Stevens: My sister, single, 28, living in Arizona City, AZ.
8. Riley Stevens: My Uncle Riley. My dad's brother. Yes, he is my favorite uncle. Always has been. Always will be. There, I said it. Lives in South Carolina with his family.
9. Tandy Gotchall: My Aunt Tandy. Yes, I was named after her. My dad's sister. Lives in California with her husband.
10. Michael Gotchall: My Aunt Tandy's husband.
11. Robert Dittrich: Maternal Grandfather
12. The Elisala family pets:

   * Roxy – Our mutt and Angel
   * Colonel – Our Great Dane and lap dog
   * Clara Belle – Our cat
   * Emma – Our cat
   * Carmine – (my mom's cat turned our cat when she died)

13. Tandy Elisala – Me!

Let the story begin, shall we?

CHAPTER ONE
The Phone Call That
Forever Changed Our Lives

"Other things may change us, but we start and end with family."

~ Anthony Brandt

T here are moments of impact that turn our lives upside down.
On December 22, 2009, at approximately 11:45am, a nurse from the Maricopa County Medical Center asked if my dad was William Stevens. My mind spun and my heart skipped a beat. "Yes, he is my dad." She then told me my dad was involved in a multi-vehicle accident and was being transported by helicopter to the emergency room. All I heard was, "you must come now!" I asked if she could tell me the extent of his injuries. She politely told me I needed to get there ASAP. I appealed to her that I needed to know if he was okay...alive...anything.... give me something! I could feel blood rushing to my head and I felt weak in my knees. She wouldn't give me any information, but asked me how long it would take for me to get to the hospital. I confirmed I'd be there in fifteen to twenty minutes. She asked me who Carolyn was and after telling her she was my mom, his wife, I asked if she too was involved in the accident. The nurse couldn't tell me whether she was or wasn't and reiterated I needed to get there quickly.

When the phone rang I was at home recovering from my own surgery just weeks prior. Sarah and Steven, my kids 14 and 16 at that time, and I jumped in the car and raced to the hospital. While driving I asked them to look up local news on their phone for any accidents being reported. Steven found it in seconds; reports of a massive accident involving over 20 vehicles on highway I-10 in Casa Grande. There were initial reports of several deaths from car and truck fires and pileups. My heart immediately sunk into my stomach, tears came to my eyes, and I could feel blood going to my head; yet, I had to be strong for the kids. I immediately took some deep breaths to calm down and continued driving, after all, we couldn't have *another* accident.

Immediate questions rushed in. Was my dad dead? Was my mom with him? Was he alone? What were our last words? What if he died and I hadn't told him how much I loved him and what a wonderful father he was?

The streetlights never seemed so long and my head kept spinning. Keep calm, Tandy. Keep calm. Minutes seemed like hours, and I couldn't get there fast enough. In an instant I realized our family roles were about to change forever and I now had to act as the head of the family.

While I was driving, my kids kept trying to reach my mom[2], but there was no answer. Where is my mom? Again, no answer. We then called my sister, Felicity[3]. More panic set in. After a few minutes Felicity called us back. Mom was at home. We told her all we knew; dad was in a car accident, we were on our way to the hospital, and that we got a hold of Amanda (my oldest daughter, 19), and she dropped everything at work to go get them.

We made it to the hospital room, and like a scene out of a movie, I was taken directly to the main emergency room trauma bay. There was my strong superman father laying motionless on a gurney with a large tag on the big toe of his right foot. Oh my God, *I'm too late*, I thought. Dad is dead.

How do I tell mom? How do I tell my sister? How do I tell the kids that he is gone? Did I tell him how much I loved him? Did I tell him that he was the greatest father I could ask for? Did I tell him how much I adored and respected him? Did he know he was my hero?

Oh my God. How would my mom face the horror and unimaginable pain of losing her husband of forty-two-plus years? Would this put her over the edge? Mom's health was already fragile. Felicity was in the middle of her own life crisis. How would she take it? My life flashed before my eyes. Who would walk Felicity down the aisle? How would my kids handle losing their grandfather in the blink

---

[2] Being disabled, my mom was unable to drive.
[3] My sister was in a leg cast as a result of her car accident the month prior and she was unable to walk or drive for months.

of an eye? My kids adored and looked up to their grandpa. He was a consistent presence in their lives and the primary person they looked to as a male figure. Oh my gosh, am I already saying "was", as in past tense? This can't be happening!

Just, then, as tears came to my eyes, I started trembling. I saw his arm move slightly, and he whispered, "My shoulder hurts like hell."

Thank you God; a miracle. I inhaled for the first time since the phone rang. Quickly relief turned to anger. Why had they placed a tag on his toe? I don't see many living people with toe tags, but television and movies had definitely convinced me that only dead people have tags on their toes.

With no time to worry about the tag, the ER doctor arrived, and not a moment too soon. He explained my dad was in an accident and still being evaluated. So far all we knew was he had shoulder and elbow injuries; in fact, his right elbow bones were grotesquely protruding out of his skin. All of a sudden, while the doctor was still with us, my dad started asking me the same questions over and over. It was obvious he was thoroughly confused; in one second, he didn't know where he was or why he was there, and the next second he would be asking for my mom, all the while telling me he hurt like hell. It was like a scene out of Groundhog Day, the loop of questions started all over again. I asked the doctor about his confusion. Is this normal? How long will this go on? The doctor replied that the confusion is very normal, particularly when someone suffered that severe a collision.

Raising my kids as a single parent most of their lives, my dad filled the gaps as their father figure, and they spent a lot of time with him. My dad encouraged everyone's education. My dad was a role model to my son Steven, and a trusting person to ask life's 'manly' questions. From encouraging education to man-to-man talks to teaching him about life, my father was there for Steven and Steven was there for my father. Steven would help my dad around my parent's house and keep my mom company, watching over her when my dad worked nights. Steven was the one who continually wanted to make the hour-long trek to Casa Grande to visit his grandparents and loved spending weekends with them. My daughters, Amanda and Sarah, also looked to my dad as a strong male figure in their lives. My father was more than just my father; he was the nucleus of our entire family, and it was never more clear when I stood over him in the emergency room.

With my dad's foot tag now removed, I went to the waiting room to get my children and let them know they could now see him. I prepared Sarah and Steven for what to expect when they saw their grandfather. I told them he did not look like or smell like their grandpa and that they would have to understand before going in that they had never seen a person in this state, let alone a relative. I explained that he was highly confused and may ask the same questions over and over and told them he was in extreme pain. With only one visitor allowed at a time, Steven was first to go see him. Thinking about what my kids were about to experience brought tears to my eyes.

I stood at the door watching as Steven stood over my dad and I felt profoundly moved by his immense sorrow, sadness, and helplessness. He tried to be brave for my dad, reassuring him that everything was going to be okay, but Steven looked as if his main lifeline was being severed from him. In that defining moment, I realized that Steven was no longer my baby boy, but a young man now. He was responsible, caring, and loving, as he watched my dad cling for his life. When Steven came out of the room, we hugged and cried together. Next it was my Sarah's turn, but after seeing her brother come out of the room visibly shaken she wasn't sure she wanted to go see her grandfather.

Her strength overcame her fear and she was determined to go see her beloved grandfather. Sarah fought back her tears, put her cell phone away (like many teenage girls, she had her cell phone attached to her ear or fingers), and took a deep breath. Sarah is not normally one to show emotions; in fact, she works hard to avoid emotional situations all together.

Watching through the doorway, when Sarah and my dad saw each other, I saw him reach for her hand and hold on tight. Sarah felt loved and scared at the same time. He asked her the same questions he had asked me over and over and over again, but thankfully I had prepared her this would happen. I was so proud of Sarah for being patient and I knew she was much more scared than she let on. She touched his arm, and then his head, and they continued holding hands. He kept looking to her for answers and wouldn't let go of her hand.

She looked over at me with tears coming down her face. I think the magnitude of the situation caught up with her when she realized he didn't remember Steven being there just minutes before, nor me a few minutes before Steven. Suddenly, she felt overwhelmed and had to get out. She wanted out...out of the room. She couldn't handle seeing her strong grandpa like that. She came out of the room crying, wiping the tears from her face and wept, *"What is happening to him? This is not okay."* I was so proud of the immense courage they mustered seeing their Grandpa in this condition. I instantly saw strength in them I didn't know they had.

My mom had not yet arrived, but after six hours and dozens of doctors, nurses, tests and thousands of unanswered questions later, dad was transferred to Barrow Neurological Institute at St. Joseph's Hospital; one of the top neurological hospitals in the world. I knew my dad would be in excellent hands and fortunately I was able to stay with him until he was transferred. But, he kept asking about mom. He still thought she was in the accident. If that was the only question he kept asking me I wouldn't be as concerned about his mental state, but it wasn't, there were many more questions. Some were serious while others were sadly funny. In fact, the confusion was so extreme at times that he thought my mom was riding side-saddle in her wheelchair! I continually reassured him mom was ok and that she wasn't in the accident.

His questions then shifted to Felicity. As I sat there listening to him talk about how he thought Felicity was in the trunk of the car and wanted to know if she was okay, my mind couldn't help but wonder would he ever be the same again. I was scared and confused myself. How someone could logically say something like that and mean it? This was all so new for me. I had never known anyone to have cognitive injuries, let alone to this extent. I wept realizing my dad actually believed Felicity was in the trunk of the car and there was nothing I could do to soothe him or snap him into reality. Seeing him in this condition made me feel helpless. All I could do was re-engage the conversation and repeatedly affirmed she was not in the accident and that she was okay. I can't tell you how many odd questions he asked, not just about Felicity. For example, my dad was so confused he also thought my dogs rear-ended the car.

The ambulance arrived and my father boarded to be transported to Barrow. Sarah, Steven and I rode behind in our car, and just as we arrived at Barrow, Felicity and my mom arrived, as if it was a scene from a movie. By this time, it had been almost 11 hours since that fateful phone call and it took Amanda nine hours to get mother and bring her to the hospital. Their arriving at the same time dad arrived at Barrow was divinely inspired, no doubt about it. The enormity of the accident kept the I-10 freeway closed; requiring Amanda to take back roads. After getting lost several times, losing cell phone and GPS reception, Amanda was exhausted, but she managed to wheel Grandma into the ER just at the perfect time! For the first time all night we were together as a family, together for each other, and together for my dad.

At Barrow, they had to repair his protruding elbow before neurological diagnosis and testing could begin. The doctors quickly took him to surgery shortly after midnight. As my entire family sat together, I sat agonizing over the magnitude and weight of the situation. My body was consumed by the sound of the wall clock second-hand beating in my head, and each minute seemed like an eternity. The hard, cold, uncomfortable chairs made waiting all the more difficult. Seconds became minutes and minutes became hours. Finally, exhausted to the point of aggravation, the surgeon came to meet us with good news. Dad made it through surgery, was in recovery, and someone would notify us when we could see him. We were still concerned, but thankful he survived surgery. Finally, at 3:30am, we visited him.

Although it was the middle of the night and dark, the sounds in his critical care room seemed very loud. Dad was hooked up to multiple machines with wires going every which way. The machines periodically beeped, giving off bright flashing sights and sounds; it was enough to give me a headache and I wasn't the one with the injuries. Not surprising, he was unconscious most of the visit so the noises didn't bother him. His skin still grey and body smelling of ashes reminded me that life is precious.

Nurses continuously came and left; each asking more and more questions, including if we had a Power of Attorney (POA) or Living Will in effect. I confirmed I was his POA, but the papers were at home. Thankfully they understood and I was asked to bring them as soon as I could.

During a few brief moments dad was lucid, we we asked him to tell us the year, but he was confused and replied sometime in the 1990's. Next we asked him about the current president, and surprisingly, he not only knew the current president and secretary of State but he even had a few choice words to say about our current political leaders. We chuckled and all took our first breath since 'the call' some 16 hours earlier. This was the first moment we all laughed as a family since the accident.

I just wanted to wake up from this nightmare, but it wasn't a nightmare; it was real and it was about to get worse. The following day, doctors discovered my dad's brain was bleeding. Somehow I was not surprised. The doctor told us it was a very serious situation and he would have to drill holes in my father's head and insert tubes and release the blood to relieve pressure, so off to surgery he went again.

During surgery doctors discovered that his colon was pushed up further than it should have been and, as a result, was accidently cut during the procedure. One would think brain surgery complications would involve his brain, but the new brain shunt they implanted required access to his abdomen. Now he had a potential life threatening infection altering recovery time after his second surgery in just a 24-hour period. And so began our new lives.

During this initial hospitalization and recovery time between December 22, 2009 – January 14, 2010, my dad continued to be very confused and appeared to lose all short-term memory. He kept asking us the same questions every few minutes and would forgot who was present. He didn't ask 'normal' questions. He asked questions such as, where his dad's house was so he could get his backpack out. Now mind you, his dad had been dead for two years. Yet somehow, he remembered details from his childhood. It was as if the last year or two of his life were gone. I was perplexed with all of his confusion. It was incredibly tough on us all physically, emotionally, mentally and spiritually. We were spent. We were hungry. In the immediate days and weeks to come, there were days we didn't bathe, sleep or eat much because we were with my dad. Everything took a back seat. We persevered and focused on my dad's recovery.

While the kids were still on holiday break, they drove my mom and sister to and from their home, our home and the hospital. While in the hospital and rehabilitation, my dad tried getting out of bed and, sometimes, he succeeded, despite IV's and restraints. He seemed to do better when family was there, especially with Amanda and me. He listened to us because of our strong personalities. He rarely listened to anyone else in the family.

Amanda adjusted her work schedule the best she could and did everything possible to be at the hospital; often going straight to work from the hospital many mornings. The vast majority of the time, Amanda and I alternated spending nights with him when he was in neurological rehabilitation, and we found his recovery to be much faster as a result. I was able to reassure my dad, and remind him to keep his sleep apnea machine on (after tubes came out of his head) and to breathe. I helped him stay in bed, and continually reminded him where he was and why he was there. In addition to giving my father peace throughout his nights, I wanted to be there for the doctor's daily rounds, which usually happened at 5:00 am. The only way that was going to happen was if I spent the night. So, I took up residence in his room.

I was still recovering from my own recent surgery and concerned I wasn't getting adequate rest. This, in part, is how Amanda stepped up for the family. Felicity was unable to be a full time partner caring for our dad because she too was involved in a recent car accident and suffered her own litany of life altering injuries; both physically and emotionally. Even given her limitations, however, she was a tremendous help with me in another way; she stayed home with mom at my parents' house so I could focus all my energies on dad. This arrangement would be short lived though because, as noted above, mom wanted and needed to be with her husband and the 120 miles round trip was not practical or possible for anyone.

To recap, I was still dealing with the emotions of almost losing my sister in her own life-threatening accident, we learned our mom had breast cancer, I was recovering from my surgery and now my dad was involved in this debilitating accident. How much can land on one person? I felt discouraged and dejected. How I would possibly handle everything before me? How could so much happen to one family? I was spiraling out of control, yet I had to fight to stay strong. I had to focus. Dad needed me as I needed him all my life.

When it rains, it truly pours. As if I wasn't dealing with enough on my over-extended plate, mom began asking me for money to pay her bills. Alarmed, I realized dad managed their money. Why had he not included mom in their money management? I became infuriated and astonished that he hadn't included my mother. Further, I learned that he spent his sizable inheritance in just one year's time, had overdrawn multiple brokerages and checking accounts, and was in considerable debt. My head was spinning. How was this happening? Where had it all gone? Did they have anything to show for it? How in the world did he blow through all this money? How would we reduce expenses, particularly now that my dad didn't have a paycheck coming in to offset the bills? Making matters worse, I knew my dad couldn't help me resolve these issues. I had to figure it all out on my own. For now, that meant me taking care of paying the bills with my money until I could digest everything.

The last week of December 2009, my dad's progress was remarkable and he was moved from critical care to a standard room. He quickly became known as "Houdini," as he would get out of bed despite being restrained across his chest, arms, and legs. We weren't completely comfortable with restraints, but after seeing blood on the floor of his room from falling, we suddenly appreciated how restraints helped and were necessary. Because his "Houdini" incidents continued, the hospital got a 'sitter'; someone who was there 24/7 in the room. This helped my dad remain safe and allowed us to eat or use the restroom without worrying he would hurt himself. We did our best to be there 24/7 from the get go but drive time alone meant he was alone for periods of time. We were glad he had a sitter.

Simultaneously, we moved my mom into our already full home because she, also, needed care. My parents lived in Casa Grande, which was about 35 minutes south of our home. The hospital my father was in was about 20 minutes north of our home. Taking all of this into consideration, mom and I agreed she should stay with us.

My dad made it through this critical time waving in and out of consciousness and having a somewhat routine schedule, if you can call it that. The hospital advised us he needed to be transferred to rehabilitation for continued care. What was rehabilitation? When was this happening? What would rehabilitation do for him and how long would he need it? Who was going to pay for this? The hospital gave me just one day to figure all this out and let them know where I wanted him transferred. I couldn't believe a hospital would put my dad in rehabilitation before, in my opinion, he was ready. Anger set it. I was angry with the hospital for their policies about transitioning patients to other facilities at certain progression points. I became angry with the person that hit my dad. Why would someone continue to drive through a massive dust storm, despite zero visibility and dangerous winds? Isn't it amazing how the impact of one person's actions can turn the lives of other's upside down? But there was no time for anger. What was done was done. The best thing I could do in the moment was focus on the task before me.

After the case manager informed me I needed to have my dad transferred and handed me a sheet with several rehabilitation facility options to consider, I asked a LOT of questions. What was the difference between acute and sub-acute care? He was a fall risk. Would facilities accommodate for this? How much does insurance pay? What exactly is rehabilitation supposed to do? What if he needs ongoing medical care while in rehabilitation? I didn't have time to be gallivanting around town touring facilities, researching and making calls, let alone feeling comfortable putting my dad somewhere within a 24-hour period. I was his advocate and felt like it was baptism by fire. But I also needed an advocate. Where was the handbook for all of this? I was scared. I was angry. I was confused. I was exhausted. I was overwhelmed.

Nevertheless, I got on the phone, did research, visited facilities and learned what I could about neurological brain injury, the difference between various rehabilitation centers, and armed myself with information necessary to make the right decisions for my dad. When I learned that the hospital had a neurological rehabilitation unit connected to the hospital, I said, "sign us up." I was all for easy and effective. The fact that Barrow's is one of the world's best neurological facilities and he would receive continuity of care put my mind at ease. I wish I would have known all my options before doing all the research I did. However, it would not be in vain as you will learn later.

With my dad now in the neurological rehabilitation unit, I insisted he be in a closely monitored room and restrained (at the arms and chest only). Through my research, I learned that acute rehabilitation facilities could use restraints. Sub acute facilities cannot. This was a deal breaker given my dad's "Houdini" tendencies. I demanded constant updates from his case manager. I asked when his caregiver meetings were, asked to be there, and consistently asked about his progress. From everything I was learning, his level of function, and his ability to effectively handle up to three hours of therapy a day—all played a key role in his level of care and to what extent his insurance companies would continue paying for rehabilitation care.

Suddenly, the burden of the entire family rested squarely on my shoulders, and despite being surrounded by family, I felt completely alone and wondered at the work of God's divine hand. I've had to deal with a lot of things in my life, but nothing, absolutely nothing could have prepared me for this.

KEY LESSONS LEARNED

1. *Be thankful and grateful for the little things in life.* We all take the 'little things' for granted; breathing, mobility, communication, just to name a few. In many ways, we need to take them for granted in order to function throughout the day. Can you imagine having to think about breathing each breath or thinking about placing each foot in front of the other to walk step by step? Certainly, being on autopilot at times is not only good, but essential. Given that, let's not forget to acknowledge and be grateful for these 'little things' for they form the backbone of our lives. As I certainly learned, one day, we could wake up and

realize these are in fact very big things. *Live each and every day as if it were your last because you never know when your last day will be*! Say I love you every single day to those closest to you.

2. *Always know and trust the immense strength and power we have within us to handle a crisis situation.* While I wasn't sure why my dad was spared his life that day or the full extent of his injuries, I soon realized the extent of my dad's strength and determination, as well as ours. I received phone calls from detectives and media outlets. As I listened to the lead detective share initial accident findings and learned dreadful details of the three deaths, I felt so thankful my dad was spared that day. While we wouldn't know to what extent my dad would recover, at least we could hold his hand, stroke his arm and head, and talk to him. I felt somber, realizing life was so delicate and there was no promise of tomorrow. In the days, weeks, months and years to come, we would just start scratching the surface of what his injuries would mean for him and for our entire family and the amazing fragility of the human brain.

3. *As much as I'd like, I can't shelter my kids from pain, nor should I try all the time.* Crisis is a real life event and how they handle it as kids helps determine how they handle crisis as adults. We must all walk our own path and there are some things we can't kiss and make better.

4. While I didn't feel or agree he was well enough to be able to come home as early as he did, *I learned and understood that insurance companies, case managers, and doctors all had goals; sometimes competing goals, causing creative tension among everyone involved in his care.* I learned that a great deal goes on behind the scenes of medical care. I didn't have any experience with care giving, so for me, I was completely overwhelmed. I would have much rather preferred he remain in rehabilitation until *after* I saw my mom through her breast

cancer surgery so I could focus on her and not have both to deal with but this was not going to happen. In my opinion, rehabilitation and hospital administrators, as well as case managers' roles are to minimize risk while maximizing profit but what's missing is the overall impact on the family. For example, I was very concerned about my father, after all the dude still thinks he's in England, and they're telling me he is ready to come home? It was then we realized rehabilitation wasn't for brain injury per se, it was for physical recovery. The rest is up to the family to figure out. The healthcare system uses a systematic methodology to determine a patient's functioning level.

5. *When a doctor or case manager says someone will need 24-hour care during inpatient care and upon being released from the hospital and/or rehabilitation, they really do mean 24-hour assistance is required.* 24-hour assistance is a great deal more than just merely preventing personal injury; it's about medications, exercises, meals, personal hygiene, physical monitoring and much, much more. Being with my dad during rehabilitation helped prepare me for what to expect at home.

6. While I was fortunate I had my dad's legal documents in order, *I needed to ensure my personal will was updated and get a durable Power of Attorney should something happen to me.* The importance of planning today for unexpected tomorrows cannot be overstated.

FAMILY ACTION GUIDE

1. We have a responsibility to our family to be a voice when our loved ones need it most; when they are unable to do so themselves. My dad couldn't speak for himself so I became his advocate. I proactively reached out to doctors, case managers, and his employer to ensure he received excellent care and everything was handled appropriately. This also meant staying

with my dad at the hospital to the extent possible. Being their voice, eyes, and ears is the best way to get full information, minimize concern, and ensure consistency of care. Particularly with brain injury, getting firsthand information was critical. As the advocate/caregiver, have pen and paper handy to take notes. This is not the time to rely on your memory! During **hospital** stays, some questions you'll want to ask the doctor(s) and other medical staff while in the hospital include:

a. What is the diagnosis? What is the short and long-term outlook and what treatments are recommended?
b. Are symptoms normal for the condition?
c. Are there any underlying concerns?
d. Will new medications be required or existing ones changed? If so, are there interactions with other medications? What side effects might there be?
e. What are the pros and cons of treatment options, as applicable?
f. What tests are being ordered and what will results show us?
g. If tests involve an invasive procedure, are there any alternatives and what are the pros and cons of these options?
h. Will rehabilitation or home health care of any kind be required? If so, what timeframe can I expect before decisions are needed? Do they have a list of preferred providers and/or facilities? Who will help coordinate needed items, therapy, supplies, equipment?
i. Before discharge, what outpatient care, prescriptions and follow up is required? When was the last time medications were given? Get specific instructions in writing.
j. When did the doctor(s) graduate from medical school and what subsequent training have they received? Do they serve on any boards, associations, or have research experience in their specialty? Do any treating doctors or surgeons have any disciplinary actions on file with the state?

    k. For surgeries, how many surgeries has the person performed? Will anyone else be operating? If so, who and why? When will you meet with the anesthesiologist? You'll want to ensure they know your medical history.

    l. What symptoms should I watch for after surgery?

    m. How long should recovery take and what does 'recovery' mean?

    n. Are there any recommended resources available on the condition?

    o. How are doctors compensated? Specifically, do they earn bonuses? If so, what are bonus-qualifying factors?

    p. How is pain management handled? Does patient need to ask for it, will staff ask for patient pain levels, or is medication automatically administered?

    q. How is discharge date determined and who is involved in the decision?

The above questions assume you don't have an opportunity to research hospitals and doctors prior to an emergency.

2. Gauge your loved one's recovery by asking non-standard memory recall questions; particularly when recovering from a brain injury or condition. Medical staff generally ask patients basic knowledge questions such as your name, the year, your location, and the current president. While these questions are good, your loved may know the answers to these because the same questions are repeatedly asked by each medical associate, but the patient may not recall their last meal, where they are or who visited them hours ago.

3. Create a patient medical and life management file system. Now, more than ever, being organized was an absolute must. As a caregiver, this is probably one of the most critical things you need to do to keep everything straight. It doesn't need to be pretty; it needs to be functional. I needed to rely on more than my memory to keep all the details and upcoming

appointments together. One thing I did immediately was get a three-inch binder and labeled the following sections:

a. Personal Information. (Name, address, phone numbers, employer name and numbers)

b. Medical Information. (Information on diagnosis, surgeries, medical history, all medications, dosages, when and why prescribed, prescribing physicians, allergies, medication side effect sheets, pharmacy information, list of hospitals, doctors and contact information)

c. Insurance. (Insurance cards, medical plan coverage overview, dental and vision plan information, short and/or long term care plan information, and insurance coverage contact information.)

d. Finances. (Bank statements, receipts, and account information.)

e. Household. (General household information such as mortgage and utility companies, account numbers, and contact information.)

f. Estate. (Copies of wills, trusts, powers of attorney, and do not resuscitate orders.)

g. Attorney/Police (For all of my father's accident related information.) At the end of each section, I had blank pieces of paper for notes within each topic/section. I then made another 1 ½" binder with sheet protectors and kept all letters/correspondence I sent out on my parents' behalf. Keeping all documentation organized will help you easily reference materials.

h. With your organized system in place, within section b – medical information, you need to have room for a *lot* of paper to ask questions and take notes before and during doctor office visits. Alternatively, you could have a notebook for taking notes and ensure the notepad fits in the organizer between appointments. Many of the questions in the hospital section in number 1 apply here. Additional questions or issues you'll want to consider discussing with all doctors:

a. Several days leading up to a doctors visit, you should write down concerns, symptoms, questions and/or changes since your last visit.

b. If given new medications, what is it, how often do I take it, what if a dose is missed, what form of medication is it (liquid, pill, capsule, syringe) and is generic available?

c. How long will the medication take to work?

d. What side effects should I look for?

e. Are there any interactions with other medications or over the counter drugs? NOTE: Pharmacists are excellent resources for drug interaction and side effect questions.

f. Are there any driving restrictions while on this medication? Does this medication have addicting properties?

g. What tests, if any, should be done to monitor condition and medication effectiveness?

h. Are there any other restrictions I should know about regarding work, lifestyle, sexual activity, diet, hobbies, alternative and integrative medicine, travel?

i. When should I follow up? If appointment is with a specialist, I'd ask when we should see them as opposed to our primary care physician.

j. Will a report of this visit be shared with (list names you want to have this information)?

k. Are there any resources you recommend on the issue(s)?

l. When should I call you as opposed to going to urgent care or a hospital?

m. If hospitalization is ever required, are you associated with and do patient hospital rounds? If not, is there a hospitalist that coordinates with the office for continuity of care?

n. Can I communicate with you and/or your nursing assistant by email?

o. Are laboratory services available on-site? If so, how long will lab results take and how will I be notified?

- p. What documentation is needed on file to ensure POA can access records as the patient can and is this listed anywhere for easy access when on the phone with office staff?
- q. How far ahead can appointments be scheduled? Do you have a reminder system?
- r. Insurance, billing and costs. This is another book entirely. On a serious note, it is important to know how much things cost, how your provider works with your insurance company and out of pocket costs. This is discussed in more detail later.
- s. If devices are sent home, such as a diabetic glucose monitor, ensure you receive proper training on how to use before leaving the office.
- t. If outside tests are needed, do I call and make appointment or will the office coordinate?

4. When faced with an unexpected health emergency, it's easy to overlook the basics. Activate all household/estate documents as soon as reasonably able in the event of an accident or illness. If you don't already have a will, durable power of attorney or a medical power of attorney, get one today. I was so consumed with my dad's immediate trauma, needs, and care while trying to stay on top of my already full plate, that a week went by before my mom said one day, "Um, the house payment needs to be made and we need money for gas." In that moment, I froze and thought to myself, *Of course you need money. Why didn't I think of that?* Had I thought of this sooner, I could have worked to locate financial accounts and get a head start executing his Durable Power of Attorney.

5. Stay calm! I know it seems silly to say but staying calm and remembering to breathe is important – not just to stay alive – but for your well being and the well being of those depending on you.

This was the beginning of my "new career" as a caregiver. Nothing could have prepared me for this role and I certainly didn't expect to be in this role at such a young age. Here I am still on medical leave from work recovering from my own surgery and I had no idea how long I would need to be on leave to care for my parents. There were so many decisions to make. There are so many stories to tell, lessons learned and advice to share. Let's move forward. While this is my story, the events, strategies, and lessons apply whether you are age 20 or 60, single or married, have young kids or no kids, live locally or at a distance, this could be your story. This could be your family. This could be you.

CHAPTER TWO
When Illness and Injury Collide

"Our family is a circle of love and strength. With every birth and every union, the circle grows. Every joy shared adds more love. Every obstacle faced together makes the circle stronger."

~ *Author unknown*

Neurological rehabilitation rooms are similar to regular hospital rooms in many ways. At our facility, dad was in a shared-room and had little space for personal items. It was different from a regular hospital setting in that there were common areas for patients to eat together and gym equipment for physical rehabilitation. It also seemed as though there were more staff around to help patients and, of course, there were more snack options for patients to have. Having extra snacks and a choice of snacks made my dad happy.

My dad received three to four hours of physical, occupational, and speech therapy daily while at inpatient rehabilitation. I immediately learned that by being with my dad close to 24/7, I could see therapy in progress and observe what they were doing and ensure treatment was being administered. This helped me immensely in preparing for his release to my home and planning for his ongoing care. Keep in mind my mom was also disabled, wheelchair bound, and on oxygen. Coming home was not a sigh of relief; rather, it opened up all new complications, just at a different location.

It became apparent that our homes had to merge. Because of my surgery recovery and push-pull weight limitations, someone else was needed to help when my mom visited my dad. With holiday break now over and my mom moved in, she visited my dad in rehab after my kids returned from school each day or I would take her and she would push herself beyond her limits by walking or pushing her wheelchair. In these instances, we would stop every few minutes for breaks while she caught her breath; we would often laugh at ourselves and the perseverance we had. We were quite creative! Sometimes, it took us half an hour to get from our car to my dad's room. By the time we would eventually make it to dad's room, we were tired and ready for a nap! I still smile thinking about the look on his face when we would walk into his room huffing and puffing and needing a rest. The upside was that dad was awake more than asleep during these visits and we could see some progress in his recovery.

Feeling discouraged and alone, my amazing, reassuring, loving, sincere and cheerful Uncle Riley visited several times. He offered respite so I could handle things at home. My head swirled with my perpetual 'to do' list of things I needed to accomplish. My heart and body, however, had a very different idea at times; sleep. I was so exhausted I was paralyzed and unable to do literally anything. At times I found myself staring at piles of papers, bills, and school notes from my kids and all I could do was sleep, cry, or stare at the growing mound before me.

Two chronically sick parents at the same time weren't in the cards. Having one parent move in is a challenge. Having two parents move in could push anyone over the edge. There were a lot of constraints on everyone; such as privacy, space and preparing my mother for her upcoming cancer surgery.

While all of this was going on, my dad continued inpatient rehabilitation treatment. He came in and out of consciousness. He was continually out of sorts. Fortunately, he consistently remembered his name, birth date, and those closest to him; like my mom, Felicity, Amanda, Sarah, Steven, and me. Dad was so annoyed and fidgety because he had trouble forming words and stringing words together to form sentences. He was confused and stewed about his inability to put the puzzle pieces together and make sense out of things. *His reality was vastly different from our reality.*

Despite my exhaustion, I continually met with his case manager, doctors, and therapists. I consider myself to have a terrific memory, but even that wasn't enough. The enormous amount of information from many different sources was like a tsunami. I quickly became a librarian; learning to document everything; keeping lists, writing questions, documenting histories; all just to stay organized. I had to keep all this information attached to my hip at all times.

Still in rehabilitation, towards the end of the first week of January 2010, a psycho-neurologist evaluated my father to determine his brain injuries, capacity and limitations. With my notebook in hand, she met with us and explained everything, including what parts of the brain were injured, what they controlled, what symptoms are likely, and the likelihood of his very limited recovery. In sum, his confabulation (the inability to remember things and short-term memory loss) would likely continue improving, but only time would tell just how much brain function would ultimately be recovered. In sum, this was 'the conversation' that he had permanently lost his ability to care for himself and provide for his family. Further, going forward, every diagnosis he received was essentially a diagnosis for the entire family.

My dad thought he was in England and some days he thought he was the king of England! Dude still thinks he is in England and the hospital released him. This is the pivotal point when we realized neurological rehabilitation wasn't focused on brain injury recovery; it was more for physical recovery. What an epiphany! While speech, physical, and occupational therapy helped and I strongly recommend it, as long as he could perform daily acts of living (such as getting in and out of bed, showering with assistance, and dressing himself) he was deemed releasable.

My father was released from rehab January 16, 2010, a few days prior to my mom's cancer surgery. While I discussed next step options with the hospital, I learned that sub-acute facilities did not allow restraints of any kind and would only provide 1 ½ hours of rehab a day rather than three hours. Additionally, insurance maximums limit the amount of time one could spend in each type of facility, criteria for acceptance into such facilities and, of course, the profit factor. After carefully weighing all the options, talking with a friend who had extensive experience in the field, and discussing this with the family, we decided that my dad should join my mom at our house and we would care for him full time. I was still on medical leave from work and in the back of my head wondered how everything was going to work out.

There was so much anticipation of my dad leaving rehabilitation and coming home with us. My dad was super excited to get outside the building and be free, and I was cautiously optimistic wondering if everything would indeed be okay. The day we left the hospital, my dad said he knew he was in Phoenix, Arizona, but his brain says he is in England. He thought all the Arizona car license plates were part of a plot and set up for his benefit. All the while, he wanted to go check on the England properties he felt he owned. Other than being thoroughly confused about everything except my mom's upcoming surgery, he was agreeable, quiet, and went with the flow. This wasn't quite who we knew him to be prior to the accident. You see, before the accident, he could be a little cranky. We also didn't know my dad to walk around in his underwear, soil himself multiple times a day, require help taking showers, require help wiping his butt, and repeating the same conversations over and over again. None of this mattered. He was my daddy. At the end of the day, I could feel how he needed to be with my mom. Similarly, I could feel how scared she was, and, despite everything, still needed him. It was just as healing for my mom to have her husband of over 42 years with her as well. They had been through a lot through life together and this was one of the most challenging health situations she had been in up to this point for them both. She needed her husband; even if he did think he was in England.

I felt completely overwhelmed and unsure how to handle caring for both a father, whom I thought should still be in inpatient rehabilitation, and my mom, who was about to have cancer surgery. Both had uncertain futures and all while I was recovering from a surgery myself. I felt like if anyone asked me anything, even directions to the bathroom, I might break. I was the ultimate multi-tasker and independent, strong woman who could do and handle anything, but this completely turned my world upside down. I no longer knew which end was up or how I was going to keep my sanity. I felt all alone, scared, and completely helpless. The last time my mother had general anesthesia was twenty-nine years prior for an emergency cesarean with Felicity and she almost died. Her health was much worse three decades later. Would she survive this surgery? Would we bury my mom when my father wasn't able to comprehend the world around him? How would her death or complications affect his healing? I felt like I was in a precarious, everlasting, and seemingly impossible nightmare.

At times through this journey, my parents would be in different hospitals across town, and I had to simultaneously be on top of both their care and prognosis. For perspective, in addition to my mom's cancer diagnosis, she had congestive heart failure, diabetes, asthma, chronic obstructive pulmonary disorder, sleep apnea, high everything and paranoid schizophrenia. She was also morbidly obese, wheelchair bound, oxygen dependent, and eventually developed stage 4 kidney failure.

The night before my mom's cancer surgery, I remember she looked so vulnerable. She looked alone, scared, and tired; yet I sensed a part of her was still trying to be strong, or at least she was putting on a brave face. My dad didn't quite comprehend what was going on with my mother, our family, or even himself. I remember watching him fall asleep, and each time his eyes made a crinkle face between his eyes signaling he was in pain. My mom really, really wanted to be in his arms. She just wanted him to hug her, she wanted to feel safe in his arms, feel the touch of a familiar hand and just be with him. He was in so much pain and his arm was very much still recovering from surgery after the accident and I felt he was consumed with this. His arm was sensitive to any pressure or touch. It was difficult for him to get how much my mom just needed his touch. As she lay next to him that night, she reached over for his hand and touched his arm. She looked at him and just rubbed his arm. She tried getting closer to him and about as far as she could get was her face being nestled by his upper arm. I felt so sad for her. I wanted to cry. I couldn't imagine facing the scariest health situation of my life and not being able to fully be with the one you love; your husband and partner for over forty-two years. I gave her a hug, told her I loved her and that everything would be okay and went to sleep.

When my head hit the pillow the night before my mom's breast cancer surgery, I prayed and cried incessantly that my mom be okay; that she would make it through surgery; through the anesthesia, through the pain, and that she wouldn't need additional treatments or a mastectomy. On January 19, 2010, at midnight, my dad and I were at the hospital with my mom for her surgery. As previously mentioned, my mom had a number of medical conditions thereby making any surgery extremely risky. She already was extremely sensitive to anesthesia so my concerns were warranted. The last time she had general anesthesia, for example, she went into cardiac arrest and was in CICU for three weeks. Despite our worries, we had confidence in her surgeon, and we knew the entire team would take good care of her and were well aware of her precarious health challenges.

When we got to my mom's hospital and talked to the doctors before surgery, I realized just how apprehensive her surgeon was about the whole thing. At first glance, I thought, if he is seriously uncertain about this surgery, that doesn't make me feel warm and fuzzy. However, as I saw him interact with her and then with us, I knew he cared deeply for my mom and wanted her to come out of the operating room alive as much as we did.

After surgery when he came to the waiting room to give us her status, I knew before he said anything that she was okay because I could see relief in his eyes. I was very, very relieved to say the least. Mom would have to stay in the hospital several more days to ensure she wouldn't experience any other complications, but the surgery was successful. Inside, I was doing a happy dance. I remember thinking, *Okay, we've gone through this hurdle. This is great. Thank you.*

We were relieved that my mom's lumpectomy was highly successful. Although she needed radiation and chemotherapy, chemotherapy was deemed too risky because of her deteriorated health conditions so we only focused on radiation and prayed for the best. We would make the trek from Phoenix to Casa Grande every morning at 7:00 am, stay at their Casa Grande home in between sessions, and return home around 6:00 pm daily. The next several months were quite challenging getting her through her breast cancer treatments.

It is difficult to put into words how overwhelmed, angry, and sad I was all the time. I had no idea how I was going to provide daily and hourly care for my dad while also taking care of my mother's recovery. Oh, and then there were my three kids, not to mention me. It's amazing how all these years being a caregiver felt like it really started when I was thirteen years old caring for my younger sister, my then husband (children's father) and, of course, my three adorable children who definitely needed me. I truly felt the weight of the world in my hands. My heart was heavy and exhausted. For example, giving your elderly father a bath and dressing him is quite an unpleasant experience at first when you are not accustomed to seeing your father naked. I knew he felt uncomfortable and embarrassed, as did I. The fact of the matter was he wasn't capable yet of doing these things himself. He needed supervision, and I was his primary caregiver.

Not only was I overwhelmed and thought it would never end, I felt guilty for putting this burden on Amanda to help me. My father's daily needs were so extreme that I felt like a bad mother at times burdening her with these adult responsibilities. If my dad is uncomfortable with *me* bathing and dressing him, imagine how uncomfortable he was having his *granddaughter* helping him. I remember my dad telling me one morning while I was putting his underwear on, "You know, I always thought that if I needed help putting my britches on, especially by my own kids, I would just go the desert and die." I felt a pain in my heart for us both, rubbed his back and said, "Dad, I'm sure this must be difficult. Please know that we'll get through this and soon you will be able to do this on your own. You wiped my butt growing up; I guess it's only fair I wipe yours now." We both chuckled and this helped lighten the mood. I will admit, though, this isn't what I had in store at this stage in our lives. Care giving is one *intimate endeavor*.

Raising three children—mostly as a single mother—I never knew I had the patience I mustered with my dad after his accident. My kids could repeat a question or statement two or three times and I would get agitated, but not with my dad. He asked the same questions over and over again in the same half hour and I would answer him as if it were the first time he asked. It was truly Divine compassion. I secretly thought to myself, *Ahhh, now I get it. I was blessed to raise my beautiful children so I could parent my parents later in life. Nice…. Very nice…. This wasn't funny!* Still, I forged ahead with incredible patience—the patience of Job from Christian Scripture.

At this point, my dad still had short-term memory loss, asked me the same questions dozens of times daily, and it was difficult for him to form new memories. Time would only tell whether he would improve. The neuropsychologist told us that the vast majority of his improvement would occur within three to six months after the accident, but then his improvement would scale back and, after one year, it would permanently plateau.

To this day I'm still not sure how we managed it all—taking an extra hour plus to get my dad ready daily, getting myself ready and getting my mom to the cancer treatments forty-five minutes away from home twice daily. I accepted that some days, I would give myself a quick sponge bath and do the same for my dad. I somehow instinctively knew how to balance everything and we made it through. I'm glad my dad was at least somewhat physically there for my mom during one of the most trying times in her life. Although he wasn't able to give care like he used to, his physical presence and loving touch was exactly what she needed from him.

Here we were at the end of January 2010. My dad continuing outpatient rehabilitation, my mom finishing intense radiation treatments and me starting to realize the possible long-term implications of care giving. I provided financial care, physical care and emotional care and wasn't sure what tomorrow would bring. Would I be able to return to work? If so, when?

KEY LESSONS LEARNED

1. *Playing the right music can really set the tone for the day.* Each morning, as we'd make the trek for mom's radiation treatments, we listened to upbeat and positive songs. We listened to everything from Cecilia's "Amazing Grace" to ABBA's "Dancing Queen". Music can be very therapeutic. When we were tired, putting on upbeat music and singing along with the chorus made for smoother, more upbeat days.

2. *Pack and take snacks for our day.* With two diabetic parents and long, nonstop days, having healthy snacks on hand was essential.

3. *Accept help.* When we are in extremely stressful situations, somehow someway, those around us rally to our support and

things seem to flow a little easier for us; from strangers helping with my parents' medical equipment to my kids stepping up and helping with more things around the house to medical personnel going out of their way to help with questions or problems. Accept help and remember to always be gracious.

4. *Never, ever, ever underestimate the power of love.* Despite logic, my dad remembered those closest to him during their darkest hours. Once he started rehabilitation, for example, he suddenly remembered my mom's cancer surgery, despite everything else being murky. Nothing was going to keep him from being with his bride of 42 years. Nothing.

FAMILY ACTION GUIDE

1. Plan meals and snacks ahead of time. Make sure there is a steady supply of healthy snacks and water on hand throughout the day helps minimize fast food urges and wasteful spending.

2. Have music appropriate to the situation and ensure all technology devices are fully charged. Starting your day with music that fills your heart, soul, energy, and body makes a profound difference to how your day goes and decisions you make.

3. ASK for support. People don't read minds. If you need help taking things to the car, ask for help. If you need help getting things in the house, ask for help. Now is not the time to be a martyr.

"There are no mistakes, no coincidences. All events are blessings given to us to learn from."
~ Dr. Elisabeth Kubler-Ross

CHAPTER THREE
Accepting a New Baseline

"Become aware that there are no accidents in our universe. Realize that everything that shows up in your life has something to teach you. Appreciate everyone and everything in your life."

~ *Wayne Dyer*

Early February 2010,

S ome baselines are okay to accept and others are not. I returned to work after being on family medical leave for 12 weeks. I exhausted my family medical leave and, at the time, honestly thought either; a) my dad would die soon or at least stay home with us and continue getting better, or b) I could handle everything and do it all well, thank you very much! Both thoughts proved futile. Just weeks later, my dad was back in the hospital for more brain surgery. After two more weeks of adding full-time work back into the mix, I realized I could not, would not, and should not be at work. Period. Walking the halls at work suddenly had me feeling something I was unaccustomed to: emptiness. For twenty plus years, every single day, even on anticipated tough days, I was full of passion, purpose, and love. I truly loved what I did, loved who I worked with and felt I made a difference. This all came to a screeching halt when I returned to work.

It was then I made the incredibly painful decision to leave a twenty-one-year career. I realized staying was unfair to everyone. I knew careers and jobs could come and go, but parents are only with us for a short time. Just one month after returning, I left my highly successful career and only form of family support. It turned out to be the right decision because between February and May alone, my dad would be in the hospital for nearly two full months. Each hospital stay, each surgery, each complication brought him a new and declining baseline. I had to face facts; my dad was a different person now. While

I could grieve for the person he used to be, I was developing an appreciation and acceptance of who he was now becoming.

Dad's abilities changed. Learning to remember short and long-term memories, how to perform acts of daily living (ADL), such as dressing himself, and retaining new information was reduced to infancy stages. The time between his initial hospital release in January and hospital stays in February were extremely difficult. Every day in every way, I felt I lost my father. Seeing him, as a completely different person was sad, yet made me happy at the same time. Although his cognitive and physical functions continually declined during this time due to multiple surgeries and the healing process itself, he became calmer and sweeter; a latent feminine side came out. Now it was easier for him to get in touch with his feelings and share them. I truly enjoyed, we all did, the serenity, peace, and calm that seemed to envelop my dad. We liked this part of him.

Unfortunately, this would be short-lived. He vacillated from being this sweet, calm man to being belligerent, angry, paranoid, and very, very confused. His neuropsychologist said this was a normal part of recovery. Still unable to form new memories, what we told him was short-lived and he would ask the same questions over and over again. He would try to fit the pieces together by taking another time period in life and adding it to his memory bank, and then believed this combined truth and reality, which was problematic to say the least. Despite this, I somehow felt patient and tolerant of my dad in his condition, even more than I would have had one of my kids asked me the same question twenty times in a half hour period.

There were many times through the journey, starting with the day of the accident, that we thought we were going to lose my dad. On several occasions, he needed help breathing and had feeding tubes. This, along with the continued brain surgeries and complications resulting from these surgeries negatively impacted his overall brain function. I can't describe how helpless I felt seeing my dad go from the highly intelligent man he was before the surgeries to the confused, angry, and paranoid man he became. A part of me contemplated why he was spared that dreadful day in 2009 if he was going to turn out this way. I learned the sad truth that brains with Traumatic Brain Injury (TBI), may improved but rarely fully recover.

More days than not, I felt helpless and hopeless, and it was all I could do to get out of the hospital cot in his room or my bed at home and put one foot in front of the other. I felt tired and exhausted; every bone, muscle, and cell in my body felt the exhaustion. There were many days I didn't want to get up. I would have given anything to be in a cocoon or my own little bubble and be allowed to rest and heal and breathe like a 'normal person'. I felt like every little thing turned into a major chore, and at times, it was extremely difficult to get through the day, let alone find joy in anything or anyone. I was depressed. Sometimes, I felt like I just wanted all the pain and sadness to just go away but the only way to do that was if I died. I must admit, at times I considered ending my life. Thankfully I realized many reasons to keep going. Probably the one thing that prevented me from going over the edge and taking such drastic measures were my children, Amanda, Sarah, and Steven. Next in line of course was my sister, Felicity, and yes, even my parents. Every time I thought things were too difficult, I thought about the immense pain and sadness they would feel about losing me, their daughter, mother, sister, friend.

I felt our family had gone through enough pain and drama and my children, my sister, my parents, and all who loved me would feel such an immense loss and losing me would put everyone over the edge. I thought about how I would feel if I lost a loved one prematurely. I thought about how we would have felt losing my dad in an instant.

I wanted to feel selfish and just go away. The pain of losing a loved one is not something I chose to put my family through. No matter what I've been through in life, I've always felt, known, and believed that I would be okay. I felt my purpose in life was to lead, heal, and teach, and I would be afforded opportunities to help thousands, perhaps millions of people someday. Most importantly, I was my children's lifeline—their rock. With an absentee father, there was no other option than to stick this out and find ways to muddle through each day. And I did just that. At first, I could only take things hour by hour, anything more was too overwhelming. Then, I gradually felt like I could handle the morning, afternoon, or evening, just not all at the same time.

There were days I vacillated between wanting to change the situation so much and have him be 'normal' again to simply wanting him to die. If he died, he wouldn't be in pain anymore, we wouldn't be on this rollercoaster, and we wouldn't have to 'deal' with all the things we had to deal with. I was angry with myself and felt so guilty for thinking and feeling this way. I felt angry with my dad for feeling like things would be so much easier if he would have died. Then, I felt immense sadness for feeling this way, and feeling grief, as if I already lost him. Each time I touched him or hugged him, I felt like Daddy's little girl all over again. I felt vulnerable, dependent, safe feelings being in his arms and I didn't want that to end.

Through all the ups and downs, I learned that I couldn't control everything. What!?! Tandy can't control the outcome? No, I couldn't change it. I couldn't be separate from it. I couldn't be at one with it— nor did I want to be at one with the situation. It took months and months of wavering between emotions of helplessness, anger, despair, hopelessness, sadness, and all these feelings again and again before I finally surrendered. My only true role was to provide peace and comfort.

Providing peace and comfort were new things to my parents. Growing up, my parents were not expressive parents; for example, they rarely hugged us. I can count on one hand the number of times my mom hugged me growing up and two hands for my dad's hugs. My parents rarely, if ever, said, "I love you." I knew they loved me, it just wasn't verbally expressed. As I grew older and got married, the dynamic of my relationship with my then, first husband was impaired because I felt stifled and didn't know it was safe to express my feelings. There are so many negative ways this played out in my marriage, but I told myself that when I had kids, I was going to tell them I love them every single day, damn it. They will always know I love them—unconditionally.

Now, decades older and feeling uncomfortable about being very expressive emotionally with my parents, I was in a quandary. Do I share my inner most feelings about my dad, our relationship, and how

I'm feeling or do I keep it inside, stay in 'thinking mode,' and let whatever was going to happen just happen. While I embraced communication with other people in my life, with my dad I felt like I was paralyzed in a way. I guess this goes to prove that it's easy for us to always think of ourselves as our parent's children and not independent adults.

It took me a week to garner the courage, to express myself. One afternoon in February 2010 while my dad was in neurological ICU when I knew nobody else would be visiting him, I decided I needed to get everything out and today was the day I was going to share my innermost feelings. I went into his room and sat next to him. My dad had been unconscious for a week at this point, without opening his eyes, he reached over and grabbed my hand and held on and didn't let go. I started crying and crying. I told him how much I loved him and how much we all loved him. I told him all the ways he was a terrific father for us. I told him that growing up, I may not have thought my childhood was great but looking back, I thanked him for providing everything he did for us and, as a mother myself now, I realize we don't go into parenthood wanting to make mistakes that would negatively impact our kids. I don't know one person who has a child saying, "I'm going to do everything I can to screw this child up!"

Suddenly, the anger and sadness of some childhood events just washed away and I released any and all negative feelings. I got to a place where there was only love...love and light. I gave him all the reasons why he should live. I gave him all the reasons it was okay to die. I wanted him to know that it was okay either way. He could stay or go. I felt a thousand times better after this and I felt we connected on a level we never had before, even though the only thing he was able to do was hold my hand. That was enough. I left his hospital room that day released from the bondage of wanting to control the situation. I learned to appreciate the ebb and flow of life and felt that whatever happened, I would be protected and guided to do the right thing.

Acceptance is really a beautiful gift for yourself. When I reached the point of acceptance, I accepted he was a different person from who he was just months prior. He would would likely never be the same again. I accepted that it was in God's hands. I just let go and I finally felt free. Accepting a new baseline means being okay with capabilities and limitations. Accepting a new baseline means letting go of the past and staying present to what it is now. Acceptance allowed me to enjoy our time together. Through this process, I learned ways to just be and be with him—the way he needed us to be there for him.

During the many stays at the hospital between February and March 2010, my father had more brain surgeries, a craniotomy to fix a brain infection that attacked his body and occurred as a result of opening his head over and over again, and TIAs, what the doctors call mini strokes. He also started having seizures. At first, the seizures were minor, but soon they became prevalent in our everyday lives. By March, he developed blood clots in his left arm and right leg. His left arm had a pick line for the IV antibiotics he needed to resolve the brain infection. Then, another mini craniotomy was needed.

There were times when my dad was conscious and times when he was unconscious. At times, I thought his memory was improving and other times I noticed his memory declining. At times, we felt he was lost inside and then times a simple smile indicated the man I knew was 'in there' and could sense his humor. I watched as my dad learned to bring out information from his brain filed away somewhere. For example, when we handed him the phone he would look at it as if it were a foreign object and he didn't know what to do with it nor could hold the phone. Regardless of the situation, we guided him every step of the way. I remember when he had the hospital TV remote in one hand, a phone rang and he put the TV remote up to his ear. And here I thought we were making progress! There were good moments too; he did remember to associate the phone ringing with talking.

Every day, I would write information on his hospital room white board including his name, date of birth, his home address, his employer name, the make and model of all the household cars, where he was and why he was there. We'd play twenty questions and I could see him trying to remember; he was thinking. Sometimes, what came out was inappropriate to the conversation, but he was thinking nonetheless. For example, one time I asked him what he had for breakfast and out of the blue he replied with another question instead and asked why we were getting US television stations if we are in

England? I explained we were not in England but he argued his point with me. There was no convincing him we were anywhere but England. There was a period of time, off and on, when he thought he was the King of England. Now, that was funny! Watching him come up with names for my kids was a hoot. He was trying to come up with Native American, English and Pacific Islander (Samoan) names for Amanda, Sarah and Steven. We were deeply touched that even in his confusion he somehow remembered our family's diverse nationalities. Go, Dad! Not even the palm trees and cactus outside his hospital window would convince him we were in Arizona. I later learned that my dad's time in England while he was in the military was one of the best times in his life. He loved his England experience. This is probably why he stayed there in his head for so long, because he enjoyed it there and felt safe.

When my dad was able to walk during his January 2010 rehabilitation, I took him slowly down the hospital halls to start gaining his energy. This was also part of his physical therapy. Each day we made the trek down the halls, he would think we were in England, Washington, D.C., a mental hospital my mom was in decades earlier, an Oklahoma City hospital, or one of many other odd places. It was like each corner of the building had some special odd meaning for him, unbeknown to us. But then at times during our walks, his mind was alert and very creative and he would ask questions about people and places that happened decades ago. The entire situation was odd to say the least. Maybe he was just trying to put puzzle pieces of life together. We will never know. At times I didn't know whether to listen to him and just let him rant or tell him the truth about where we were at that point in time. I decided to rotate between the two strategies and watch for trends on which strategy worked best.

As I attended to my dad's speech, physical, and occupational therapy sessions, I watched as his therapists corrected him when he was going down an incorrect path. Then I would proudly witness my dad responding to therapy as he relearned how to use a telephone, dial numbers, and remember whom he was calling and for what purpose. This was a period of mixed emotions for me because these were basic tasks an elementary school child knows how to perform. I felt helpless watching my dad relearn such basic things and felt so sad for him, as I could see the frustration in his face and throughout his entire body as he tried to grasp concepts of time and money; just to name a few.

Some facts my dad almost routinely recalled included his name, birth date, his wife's name, and her birth date. However, during his darkest hours, he couldn't say these things and became extremely angry that he couldn't say or remember his own name. Despite this, I never gave up on him. And often when the doctors and nurses called his name and when he was conscious, he responded to them. Another example of how I knew he was still present was when the nurses would do neurological checks. Part of this process involves them asking him to perform certain functions: hold a fist, push against their hands with his feet, open his eyes and follow their finger, and the like. Normally my dad would not respond to anyone but Amanda or me so the doctors loved it when we were there for these checks because we helped them get the information they needed to assess his true condition. I would ask him to open his eyes and wham—he'd open them...at least most times. Sometimes, however, he would immediately close them or they wouldn't open. Dad seemed to followed my verbal commands when he was conscious, and when he wasn't conscious and I would ask him to hold my hand tight, he would almost always follow this command. Yes my dad was still my dad. His recognizing my voice was very reassuring.

On the way home from hospital trips in February 2010, my dad would say, "Okay, the streets and buildings tell me we are not in England but my brain tells me we are in England." True to form, he hypothesized how the England hospital and Arizona hospital had a partnership and we were just across the river. And we just agreed. After all, it was our new baseline.

KEY LESSONS LEARNED

1. *The brain is a complex organ.* Doctors can't fully explain its ability and why some people heal and others don't. Never

underestimate this powerful organ! The brain, combined with determination, goes a long way towards healing.

2. *The power of our minds transcends human understanding.* Our physical bodies are absolutely amazing. Sometimes, without warning or explanation, our bodies defy modern medicine or logic and recover in amazing ways. Don't count people out until the heart permanently stops.

3. *I had to learn what I didn't know.* There's a difference between knowing what you don't know and not knowing what you don't know. There was so much information I needed to have at my fingertips and it took time finding it or information wasn't readily available and I developed my own system to figure it all out. This is one of the biggest reasons I wrote this book. If there is one thing you learn from each chapter you can carry with you, all the hard work was worth it. Evaluating care needs, options, insurance, who the authority was on what, what to consider in determining where my dad should go and the pros and cons of each option were all things I learned along the way.

4. *I realized that what I was experiencing as a caregiver and daughter was normal and was exactly where I needed to be.* I recalled someone telling me years ago that we never get 'over' things; we get 'through' them. This is so true. Remember that there is always a way through a situation, even if you don't see it at the time. When you feel you just can't go on and that nothing will help and you begin thinking you would rather die, please, please, please seek medical attention immediately. Help is always available and in many different forms. There is no contest for sucking it up, so to speak. You must take care of yourself before you can effectively take care of others. When I felt such despair and realized I needed help, I sought it out.

FAMILY ACTION GUIDE

1. Be a proactive partner in your loved one's medical care and evaluate all care options as soon as possible. Keep tabs on how the hospital and insurance is evaluating their progress and be on top of and plan for post hospital care *now*. This is so critical. You must be their advocate and understand their limitations and needs. You've got to understand the right people to ask the right questions of in the medical community.

2. Determine your care giving readiness on all levels. Everyone should work *with* your loved one in determining level and types of care needed. What's going to work for everyone in the family? In home, multi-generation home, home health care, assisted living, long-term nursing care. For assisted-living options, how will you assess their financial, physical, emotional, mental, spiritual considerations and ensure ongoing safety is met?

3. When my dad was going through his first rehabilitation stay, I would have brought more family photos to the hospital much, much sooner than I did. We brought pictures after his first hospitalization. Had he and his rehabilitation team had family photos during his first stay, it may have helped put puzzle pieces together sooner. Better late than never because it did help my dad remember things, helped us determine how he was healing, promoted storytelling among us, and helped us appreciate our family that much more.

4. Research. Research. Research. If you are going to seek legal counsel or move a loved one into a short - or long-term nursing/assisted living facility, you must do your research before interviewing others and making decisions. Doing your research makes you a better advocate, care giver and medical team partner and it prevents you from being taken advantage of or making costly mistakes. Whether you are preparing ahead of time or facing immediate patient transfers, listed below are important topics and questions to consider.

a. <u>Insurance Coverage</u>. What are the medical and payment limits? What is considered in-network vs. out of network and what are the limitations and deductibles of your specific plan(s)? Are doctors and specialists covered in network if they are seeing patients in an in network facility or are doctor bills considered out of network if they are part of a hospitalist group coordinating care? If you have multiple insurance plans, which plan in primary and which is secondary? Do *they* know this? Most people think having multiple insurance plans mean less out of pocket expenses. For us, it meant insurance companies pointing the finger at each other claiming the other insurance carrier was primary. It meant countless hours on the phone with coordination of benefits to continually update their ever-changing systems. It also meant frustration, time, paper, stamps, invoices, account receivables and possible collections activity because the insurance companies can't 'get along' and pay the darn bills.

b. <u>Doctors</u>. Are doctors contracted with this particular facility? Is there a hospitalist coordinating care? What are the on-call and weekend schedules? Are back up physicians part of the same group? How are quality of care and communications? Who is allowed in operating rooms? Who is actually performing procedures/operations? Are all patient notes automatically shared with their primary care physician's office or is this something you must do yourself?

c. <u>Level of care</u>. Does the facility have anticipated equipment on site or a relationship with such a provider for continuity of care? How quickly do we get test results? (This includes labs, testing equipment and pharmacy.) In our case, for example, any facility needed to have CT and MRI capability.

41

   d. <u>Nursing</u>. What is the nurse-to-patient ratio? For assisted
       living facilities, what is the staff turnover rate? What times
       of day are shift changes? Is there continuity of
       communication and care? Does the staff look happy? How
       are medications managed and documented? How often are
       patients checked on? Who else is part of the nursing care
       team? Are there Certified Nursing Assistants (CNA)
       available? How effective is communication between
       nursing and other departments? Would nurses put their
       loved ones in said facility? Why or why not?

   e. <u>General Conditions</u>. Is the facility clean? Are there any
       complaints with the state and, if so, what is the nature and
       resolutions of the complaints? What is the overall
       friendliness of the staff? Did you observe good safety
       protocols? Are patient rooms clean? Are single rooms
       available? If so, are they at the same price point? If not,
       what is the room set up for shared rooms and access to
       needed supplies, bathroom, and thermostat, for example?

   f. <u>Visitor and Technology Policies</u>. Are visitors allowed 24/7
       access? Can we stay the night? If so, is there a bed, cot or
       chair; or could we bring our own sleeping 'gear'? Is there
       free, accessible and reliable internet and phone service?
       Are meals available for family members, and if so, how
       much did they cost? Was there a family meal order
       deadline? What is security? Is the administration accessible
       at all times? Are medical records electronic, paper or both?

   g. <u>Visit the cafeteria</u> and listen to conversations. You'd be
       surprised what you can learn about doctors, nurses,
       administration, staff quality, employee engagement and
       food quality!

5. My dad took painstaking time documenting his life history
    several years prior to his accident. Little did we know this
    information would prove to be key in aiding medical and

rehabilitation staff with his brain memory recall. Here are the categories and lists my dad documented:

a. A chronological life list of all addresses up to and including his home at the time of the accident.

b. A chronological list of employers, job titles, locations, supervisor names and salaries.

c. His military deployment locations and dates.

d. All personal and professional associations he belonged to, their websites, login and password information.

e. All websites, login ID's, passwords and secret words for every place he did business.

f. All life insurance policy names, addresses and amounts.

The first three lists were worth every single moment he spent putting them together for rehabilitation purposes. His medical care team was able to help him put pieces together, determine fact from fiction and guide conversations accordingly. For example, you can probably guess by now that my dad loved England. The time he spent there in the military was probably the best time of his life. He retreated there after the accident because it was safe and it was his happy space. It was also because he was highly confused. With the rehabilitation team knowing personalized details of his time and places, they were able to determine if what he was saying was true or not. The rehabilitation team thanked me profusely for sharing this with them and said they wished every patient had these types of records. The last three lists were worth every single moment for my purposes. I was able to piece things together from the list, mail received, bank statements and such and take appropriate action.

6. Allow your loved one to be who they are. Be patient and refrain from trying to change or criticize them. Nobody is more

frustrated about being unable to walk, talk or form thoughts than the person going through it. No matter how hard it may be to want to jump in and talk for them, remember silence is golden. Lastly, always talk as if the patient can hear and understand you.

7. Look for signs of depression and get professional help if you are feeling depressed for an extended period of time. Brain chemistry can change after prolonged depression and can be more difficult to treat without professional help. If you have thought about hurting yourself or others, seek IMMEDIATE MEDICAL ATTENTION. Mental health is just as important as physical health and needing to seek help is more common than you realize.

Signs of depression include and aren't limited to:[4]

- Feelings of sadness or unhappiness
- Irritability or frustration, even over small matters
- Loss of interest or pleasure in normal activities
- Reduced sex drive
- Insomnia or excessive sleeping
- Changes in appetite — depression often causes decreased appetite and weight loss, but in some people it causes increased cravings for food and weight gain
- Agitation or restlessness — for example, pacing, hand-wringing or an inability to sit still
- Irritability or angry outbursts
- Slowed thinking, speaking or body movements
- Indecisiveness, distractibility and decreased concentration
- Fatigue, tiredness and loss of energy — even small tasks may seem to require a lot of effort
- Feelings of worthlessness or guilt, fixating on past failures or blaming yourself when things aren't going right

---

[4] mayoclinic.com

- Trouble thinking, concentrating, making decisions and remembering things
- Frequent thoughts of death, dying or suicide
- Crying spells for no apparent reason
- Unexplained physical problems, such as back pain or headaches

"40% to 70% of family caregivers have clinically significant symptoms of depression with approximately a quarter to half of these caregivers meet the diagnostic criteria for major depression."

~ Zarit, S. (2006). Assessment of Family Caregivers:
A Research Perspective

CHAPTER FOUR
Balancing Moving Parts

"If you are headed in the wrong direction, God allows u-turns."

~ *Author unknown*

My house in a Phoenix suburb is a modest four-bedroom/two-bath home with a living room and family room. When moving my mom in with my three kids, Berlin, a friend of my daughters' who needed help, two dogs, two cats, and me, it was quite the experience. Mid February 2010, we converted the family room into a hospital/everything room for my parents. Somehow, we dealt with a new schedule that included bathing my dad, a myriad of doctors' appointments, and laundry pileups around the house, a rotating car schedule, a bedside potty, and a complex medication schedule. My artwork was replaced with a white board on the wall containing our daily schedule and basic information for my dad to help him remember basics; such as his name, the date, and his hourly schedule. This chapter delves into blending my parents into an already full household of my kid's schooling, football, Job's Daughters (a girls' fraternal youth organization), and my career.

The anticipation of having to provide intense 24/7 supervision for my dad and provide full time care for my mom was very overwhelming. When I say intense 24/7 care for my dad, I mean *intense*. I fed him, helped him to the bathroom, wiped his behind, cleaned up accidents, made and changed his bed, kept all fourteen medications straight, kept on top of his blood sugar and insulin needs, and helped him around the house at all times. He could not be alone and needed help dressing, bathing, eating, etc. He was still unable to form new memories and remained very confused about everything. Every single day, I was answering the same questions again and again; it was no wonder I could finish his sentences when he couldn't. He would say a few words—not even in order— and I understood what he was saying or asking. I remember asking him to nod or put up a finger with his good arm if I was on target. Ninety-nine percent of the time, I was right on. I knew my dad so well.

There were times over the next several weeks that I felt overwhelmed with intense fear. Then exhaustion set in. I remember feeling so overwhelmed and sad. I was literally paralyzed in virtually every other area of my life. Breathing, living and sleeping around my parents' care was literally all I could do. To think about the simplest of tasks or other responsibilities was just too much to bear during this time. There were times I thought I was close to a breakdown. I simply couldn't shake the emotions and if it didn't involve my family—I had no room for it in my energy field. On top of this stress, I had just been through a divorce from my second husband.

Just as we were settling in from my dad's February hospital discharge, his condition again deteriorated. Mid March through May 22, 2010, my dad was hospitalized for various complications resulting from the accident and subsequent brain trauma. There were times we thought we would lose him and each time, he came through. Each time he overcame a new challenge he had a new and declining baseline level of functionality. This proved difficult for everyone to handle, especially my dad. As he was able to start forming and retaining new memories, he became increasingly agitated, sad, and determined all at the same time.

While one or both of my parents were in various hospitals between March 2010 and May 2010, I realized I needed to focus my attention on practical matters like selling their Dallas, TX rental home. I also needed to empty out their two storage rooms in Casa Grande (where they lived prior to the accident), either rent or sell another property my dad bought months before his accident, and figure out our options with their primary residence. The rental property was completely filled with what I call 'stuff'. A lot of stuff. Then there was the matter of what to do with their household goods in yet another very large storage room in New Hampshire.

Without a steady income, my parents could not afford any of their homes or storage units. You might be thinking, *My goodness they sure had a lot of 'stuff' to fill three (3) storage rooms, one (1) rental home in addition to their primary residence*—and you'd be right! My dad kept everything just in case he or someone else needed it. Making matters worse, my dad forgot what he kept and where he kept it. My dad always collected a lot of stuff, but it really became a serious problem over time. I remember growing up, my mom would keep our house clean and clear of clutter in the visible living spaces and confined my dad to certain bedroom space for his 'stuff'. It seemed manageable then. Over the years though, I think my mom felt resigned to it and gave up trying to keep the house organized. Now, handling all their 'stuff' became a huge burden and a family affair.

I made a plan, and during spring break of March 2010, Amanda, Steven, and I left for New Hampshire to clear out the dreaded ten-year-old storage unit. My dad was in the hospital and I felt he was 'stable' enough to leave for a week. Felicity and Sarah stayed to care for mom. My aunt and uncle strongly recommended we just have the storage unit owners chuck or donate everything, as they didn't think there would be anything of value if it wasn't looked at in ten years. Normally, I would agree. However, back then, my dad was responsible for most of the packing and storing things away as they abruptly and suddenly found themselves moving to Arizona to help me and my kids through a tumultuous time during my first divorce. The problem with this 'just toss it' theory is my mom was adamant that our hundred-year-old family china and silver set were in storage, along with with several lamps made by her mother, frames and art that meant a lot to her, a Chinese jewelry box my Grandpa (her dad) gave my mom early on in their marriage, military items and jewelry.

I remember the first day we arrived at the storage facility. The owners cut the lock open for us, and as we raised the door, the three of us stood there with facemasks and gloves on, just staring at the overwhelming job ahead of us. It felt like a scene from *Ghostbusters*, when Dan Aykroyd, Bill Murray, and Harold Ramis were frozen from realizing the monumental task ahead of them. Box by box, item by item, we went through each and every item in each and every box. We took countless trips to the city dump, called local charities to pick up some things, and repacked a total of thirty-one boxes to ship home. Of the hundreds and hundreds of boxes, we managed to find everything on my mom's list; we felt accomplished. We knew that taking care of this would put my parents' minds at ease, as it was something they've wanted to do for many years yet life events superseded these plans.

We had fun taking boxes back to our hotel room and going through all the memories before repacking and securing for transport. The hotel, however, wasn't quite sure what to make of all the boxes and things coming and going. As if we weren't trying to cram enough tasks in a short time, the bad weather didn't help; it rained three of the five days. Our last day in NH, we made ten trips to the local post office and mailed all thirty-one boxes home. There were some things too precious to mail; such as all our family photos (including my parents' photos and our baby and childhood photos), my dad's military stripes and honors, and many other family mementos and service awards. My mom's precious family jewelry also flew with us via carryon. TSA wasn't sure at first about letting us go through security with all the 'metal', but, after I explained the situation and they thoroughly checked everything, we were on our way.

On the flight home from New Hampshire, Amanda quietly and reflectively expressed her excitement anticipating Grandma's reaction of being reacquainted her precious belongings. I was so proud of Amanda, and she seemed so content having accomplished a great deal that week. She and I think a lot alike, and sometimes, she verbalizes exactly what I am thinking. I can't describe my emotions when we returned home watching my mom as Amanda and I handed her everything she had on the list. As I've mentioned, my mother is not a verbally expressive person; I've seen her cry and get emotional maybe five times in my entire life and three of these times were since my father's accident. Witnessing my mom shake and cry holding her family jewelry, our hundred-year-old family silver set, my sister's baby pictures, and her wedding album made all the bumps, bruises, sore muscles, sleep deprivation, broken prescription glasses, and hard work worth it. When we took some of the items to the hospital and showed my dad, he too became emotional and seemed very content knowing we cared enough to go through everything and find these 'lost' treasures. The funny thing about finding our family heirlooms was the silver set was packed in four different boxes with things that had nothing to do with each other. For example, some boxes had books, floppy disks, Tupperware, and napkins; others had empty coffee tin cans, taxes, tablecloths, and candles. That's my dad for you. This, we discovered, was par for the course for him. There was no obvious method to anything he kept, bought, packed, or labeled.

After we returned home from New Hampshire, we addressed their houses and first thing we did was immediately sell their Texas rental home. I instantly learned how to become a property manager. Then I rented out the other home my dad was using for storage to a handyman we met when going through their two local storage rooms. Vince, the handyman, was so kind and helped take things to the dump. He was a single father struggling to provide for his son, and was honest, hardworking, and ethical and cared about doing a job the right way. It's amazing how the right people came into our lives at just the right time, and I'm so grateful we were able to help him as he had helped us. Eventually, we sold the property he rented, yet it was important to us that we would only sell it to someone who allowed him to buy the home in the future when he was ready.

Between January and March 2010, Felicity and Vince did most of the work clearing out the two local storage rooms. Anyone with a storage unit knows this is no small or easy task. Even though Felicity was still recovering from her car accident, she helped tremendously and spent countless hours sifting through more, endless boxes. Among the findings were over six (6) photo albums, family letters written generations ago, and previously unknown family diaries. As soon as the storage rooms were cleaned out, we focused on tackling their primary residence in Casa Grande.

It would take six (yes, *six*) large mini mobile units to clear everything out of their home. By the the end of our time clearing out their house, my dad was released from the hospital (May 22, 2010) and he wouldn't let us get rid of anything more without his input. He became highly agitated and paranoid about clearing out his stuff. It was sadly fascinating to us that he couldn't remember the day or what happened five (5) minutes ago but he knew what we throwing away in the trash. I guess I could see his point. As someone who treasures my belongings, I too would be agitated if people began tossing my stuff and making decisions about what to do with my things without my feedback. Fortunately and to our credit, my mom wrote down a list of things they needed and we used that list as the basis for many decisions.

Some of my parents' belongings went to Felicity's house, some to our house, and many things were donated or thrown out. One thing my very wise daughter, Amanda, and Felicity, helped me realize through this process, was that getting rid of their 'stuff' without their presence, active participation, and agreement just made the situation worse. I'm grateful for this insight. Eventually all of their belongings from all the storage rooms and homes across the country were now in our living room, which in effect became their living space. I can only imagine the lack of control they felt. We successfully sold their primary home through a short sale and towards the end of summer 2010, my stress level started decreasing. Things seemed temporarily manageable.

Throughout this process so many emotions came over me. I was angry that I worked hard to have a clutter-free home and all of a sudden I was now knee-deep in their stuff. How is this fair? I resented my dad many times for living his life this way. Then, I became sad that my parents felt so out of control in their lives that they felt they needed to keep things to that extent. I wondered how and what happened in my dad's life that made him hold on to every little item in his life. I felt a real struggle between feeling better we were getting this 'task' off of the list and seeing their visible sadness about their world being pushed aside and turned upside down.

Feelings aside, from a practical matter, there was a sense of urgency to get this done for many reasons. First, I wanted to get as much cleared out before my dad either got out of the hospital or passed away; it was still touch-and-go for many months and my time would need to be redirected towards him. Since they had two homes at the time and it was clear they likely would not be able to live on their own again, I felt a tug of war inside between our sanity and their fears. Because we weren't attached to their 'stuff', it was much easier for us to let go of these things. At the time, my objective was reducing expenses, simplifying, and preparing for the future. I felt absolutely horrible they weren't able to see, touch, and approve all actions with their things. I felt conflicted and had to make the better of two rough choices. I don't know which would have been harder: clearing their belongings while they were alive or waiting until after death.

Balancing moving parts under the best of circumstances can be difficult but this took things to a whole new level. For example, during this time, we also put one of my parent's cats to sleep. Any pet owner knows how traumatic this is, especially for ill, homebound people. Because I already had our own little farm of animals, the house could only handle one more pet; and that was a stretch. Fortunately, Felicity stepped in and agreed to take one of mom's cats and we took one cat, so mom was happy that they were all being loved. This was a huge sacrifice for me because we already had two cats, one of whom is blind, deaf, and extremely anxious about change, and two dogs—our beautiful mutt, Roxy, and our Great Dane, Colonel.

On top of that, my daughter Sarah's friend, Berlin, needed a place to stay because she was failing school and needed a loving home. I allowed her to move in with us, sharing a room with Sarah, provided she abides by my family rules. She lived with us the rest of 2010, and eventually moved in with her dad in January 2011. I am proud to say she earned her first "A" grade while living with us. We were so proud when she graduated high school.

Our household seemed to have an active revolving door. Just as Berlin moved out, Felicity moved in for 30 days. Felicity had her second car accident in only two months. This time she was convicted of Driving Under the Influence (DUI) for prescription medication. As a result, her license was suspended. Since she lived in a city with no mail or bus service this posed a few issues. She needed to live closer to work because she now needed to be driven to and from work daily. Planning another person's daily commute was another unexpected moving part. Thankfully, after her suspension she was able to drive with restrictions and thankfully, her car was now repaired. There was never a dull moment in our home. It brings a whole new meaning to the term, "one big happy family." In all seriousness, this took much loving support by and for all and was not easy at times.

Six months had passed. The time had come for me to think about returning to work. When I left my job to care for my parents, we honestly didn't think my dad would be alive to see summer and thought it was really important to allow my parents to live and die in dignity together. As summer ended, however, Amanda and I agreed that she would assume the primary caregiver role so I could go back to work. This was a tremendous sacrifice for a young woman in two ways. First, assuming a care giving role at such a young age when most 19-year-olds are enjoying a more carefree, fun life. Second, postponing college indefinitely is an extremely selfless act. I don't know what I would have done without my kids through all of this.

It wasn't even two weeks into my job search when a previous boss I had worked with many years prior called me about possible opportunities in his organization. Shortly thereafter, I started my new career and was so thankful the universe unfolded with just the right opportunity at just the right time.

Balancing a divorce, my parent's hospital stays and surgeries, unemployment, my dad's declining health, new animal additions, moving, moving, more moving, rearranging and purging my home to accommodate my parents, my own health issues, daily responsibilities as a mother, countless doctor's appointments, Felicity's growing addiction to medication and personal health challenges is about as high on the stress list as one can imagine. Any one of these things can negatively affect one's overall well-being, let alone a combination of moving parts. This is where the importance of self-care played an integral part of my life and my family's life. The next chapter describes ways I took care of myself while balancing these moving parts and came out the other side stronger for it.

KEY LESSONS LEARNED

1. *I carried a master calendar with me at all times.* I incorporated every single event for everyone in the household in my master calendar. I knew when to get the animals vaccinated and when to give the dogs' heartworm medication. I knew when to change the house air filters. I knew when it was time for car oil changes. My kids' school events, medical testing days, meal

planning, and the ever-popular doctor's appointments were on the list. It took some planning time up front, but it was well worth the investment. This helped release my mind of all these things and allowed me to focus on the important stuff.

2. *I started posting our weekly family calendar on the refrigerator every Sunday for the following week.* Everyone was able to look at the week at a glance and my dad could (and did) refer to the daily schedule on the refrigerator multiple times a day. Anytime he asked me something about the schedule, I referred him to the kitchen. It took awhile for him to remember this, but he eventually was able to form new memories and get there by himself.

3. *I kept a journal and blog* to write happenings of the day, my feelings about the day/week, and my sister kept a journal of funny things our dad would say or do so we could remember and tell him about it later. This helped negative feelings from festering and was a form of release.

4. *Removing physical signs of 'hoarding' only redirects the behavior.* This is a serious issue requiring professional help. We thought we were doing a good deed and, yes, there was urgency around cleaning things out; however, this is not how I would recommend handling these issues going forward. As time passed, I realized how someone with a lifetime of behavior will find a way to continue the pattern; one destructive way or another.

5. It is important that key information be updated for all family members and medical personnel. We had this list and everyone had copies. With Amanda becoming more of a full-time caregiver, we needed to ensure all information was updated regularly.

FAMILY ACTION GUIDE

1. Anticipating and accepting moving parts makes things more manageable. There will always be moving parts of some kind happening around us.

2. Start a master schedule pronto! For the first few months, I was the go-to person for any question about anyone and anything on the schedule. When I realized I could reduce my stress and save time by publishing everything weekly, I felt free and wondered why I hadn't thought of doing this sooner.

3. Write down key events throughout the process. Record progress and key events. You never know when or how you'll need it. Perhaps, you'll even write a book someday and this information can help you on your journey.

4. Maintain an updated list of the following:

   - All medications
   - Dosages
   - Reason for taking medication(s)
   - How long you've been taking medications
   - Allergies
   - Health conditions
   - Surgeries and dates of surgeries
   - Insurance information including a copy of the front and back of insurance cards and ID cards
   - Medical and Durable Power of attorney documentation. Have all driving family members keep a copy on their person and in the car. Should something unexpected happen, emergency personnel need this information and the sooner they have it, the better they can care for your loved one.

5. Although not specifically discussed in this chapter, I felt guided to include an action item regarding out of town trips. My mother

had an oxygen concentrator for home, a portable concentrator for on the go, a sleep apnea CPAP machine, a wheelchair and other sundry items needed at any given time. Here are some tips for traveling with people who have 'moving parts':

- Work with your insurance company to coordinate delivery of medical supply equipment to the traveling location. We were pleasantly surprised to discover that a home oxygen concentrator could be delivered to an out of town hotel. In our case, the concentrator was in the room before check in and the local home health care company picked up the equipment upon check out. Everything was easy as pie in this circumstance. Unfortunately, we were traveling for a funeral so it wasn't a pleasure trip. It was nice to know that insurance companies can coordinate these things.
- Determine what disability resources are available while out of town, as needed.
- Contact businesses you know you will visit and ensure they accommodate your specific needs. In one case, a family gathering was in a location that didn't have easy access for wheelchair bound people. Legalities aside, this is an important thing to know ahead of time.
- Contact airports, bus stations or train stations you are traveling with and schedule needed assistance ahead of time. Having an employee help navigate through the traveling process can significantly reduce stress.
- Plan extra time for unloading and loading of items and getting through security checkpoints.
- Advise security personnel of any medications, equipment or devices ahead of going through security. Label everything and have doctor's notes (if the prescription isn't clear on said medication bottle) as needed, for any medications that fall outside of traveling standards such as the maximum liquid allowances.

CHAPTER FIVE
The Importance of Self-Care

"The Inner cadence of contentment we feel when the melody of life is in tune. When somehow we are able to balance the expectations and responsibilities in the world on one hand with our inner need for contentment on the other. Sometimes, we neglect the thing we need most: quiet reflective time. Time to think. Time to dream. Time to realize what's working and what's not...take time to pause...."

~ Sara Buchanan

This chapter addresses one of the most important aspects of care giving: self-care. In fact, self-care is critical for a person's overall well-being, whether or not you are a caregiver. If you aren't taking care of yourself it is impossible to effectively take care of another; despite what you may think. Sure, your body may go with the flow for awhile and then... something happens and your physical and emotional well-being becomes jeopardized. Without a doubt, our ability to care for others in any capacity is directly proportional to our own overall health. Yet, often, the thing we need most, such as adequate rest and right nutrition is the thing we put to the side and consider a 'to do' item. When we need to slow down and care for ourselves, we often get caught up in the hustle and bustle of life. The degree with which I handled everything through this entire journey was directly proportional to the degree with which I practiced effective self-care. Some things I got right, and others I got wrong. My sincere hope is that you learn from my experiences and capitalize on the things I did well.

I found that when I got off track, my health suffered so I reached into my arsenal of tools and aimed to preserve my well-being. Core things I never compromised included my meditation practice and prayer. Some days, it was for five minutes and other days, an hour. When I slept on hospital cots or chairs and generally ran around like a chicken with my head cut off, meditating helped to slow my mind and keep me centered. Through my personal trials and tribulations, over time, I overcame feeling guilty doing things for me when there was so much to do for everyone else. It was tough putting me first when I felt helpless and paralyzed at times and just wanted to stare at the TV or the sky. Developing and maintaining consistent self-care strategies were particularly difficult, as I had been accustomed to caring for others most of my life.

> *"If I am not good to myself, how can I expect anyone else to be good to me?"*
>
> ~ *Maya Angelou*

There are so many aspects to self-care. I've organized this chapter by things I did well, opportunities for improvement and a personal action guide. Note that I said personal action guide rather than family action guide. This chapter is for YOU.

Here is a list of things I did right.

1. I learned how to sleep anywhere, such as in chairs and on cots. I was never one to be able to sleep in an upward position or on hard surfaces, yet acquired this new skill.

2. I consistently maintained my daily meditation and prayer practices. I believe giving thanks is a tremendous way to receive more of what we're thankful for and bring this into our lives. Meditation and prayer were my mainstays—those things I did not and could not do without. Whatever daily practices or traditions you have, I urge you to just do it, stick with it, and forget what's going on around you for that amount of time. Whether you have five minutes, fifteen minutes or an hour, make a dedicated time -your sacred time.

3. Get out of bed. Some days, just putting my feet on the ground and getting out of bed was an accomplishment.

4. Maintain personal grooming care. I'll admit it took me a while to overcome little twinges of guilt for taking time to get my hair cut and highlighted when there was SO much to do and so many bills. But when I did keep up with these things, I felt better. I felt like my batteries had been recharged. A few hours to yourself are all you need to get you back to this centered space. I blocked it off my schedule and did my best to keep my personal appointments. It may seem like such a little thing, but when your hair or whatever part of you that is important to you (whether it's shaving, waxing, manicures, etc) gets neglected, it can negatively change your outlook on life. I found doing little things, like taking just thirty seconds to rub lotion on my hands, was sometimes all I needed to help me feel good inside. When we feel good inside, we feel better equipped to handle daily stressors.

5. I periodically treated myself to manicures and pedicures. Local schools teaching this occupation often provide these services at a deep discount.

6. Take a walk. even a ten-minute walk around the block was refreshing. Sometimes, when at the hospital, I would go outside, walk around, and be with nature for a few minutes.

7. I read books. I love reading. I always carried a book with me in my purse. I found myself better able to handle delays and the waiting game that often happens in hospitals, ER's, waiting rooms, and doctors' offices. Reading was me time. Now, I see that what I read actually helped me be a better leader, parent, daughter, wife, and friend in addition to helping me maintain patience.

8. I learned to let go of the little things. Sometimes it takes something big like an illness, disease, accident or injury to our selves or loved ones to make us realize that the little stuff doesn't matter; it generally takes care of itself. For example, I used to be pretty stressed if all the dishes weren't done, the counters weren't wiped off, floor weren't swept, etc. I have since realized that the dishes can wait. I learned to look at life

through a new lens and with new primary questions, "If I died tonight, would the dishes matter? If something happened to one of my kids or other family member, would the floor matter?" If the answer is NO, of course not, then let it go. If I'm tired or just don't feel like doing whatever it is that needs done, I am really okay leaving it for another time.

9. Ralph Waldo Emerson said, *"Health is the first muse, and sleep is the condition to produce it."* I slept in some days despite feeling like I had too much to do. This body has reminded me in recent years just how powerful sleep is to our overall health and well-being. Having my share of health issues and an immune system that has yet to get the perfect health memo, I definitely notice when I don't get enough sleep. Some people can live on two, three, or five hours of sleep. I can go one night with less than eight hours of sleep but I pay for it the next day. If I don't get enough the second night, my body physically feels it and I start getting ill. To accommodate, I learned to take naps during the day. Sleep and uninterrupted sleep are two different types of sleep. I was blessed to have Amanda and Felicity to help rotate hospital duty with my dad so I could squeeze in necessary sleep.

10. I took time to watch funny movies, motivational movies, and lighthearted shows. Sometimes, I just wanted to watch something on TV that didn't require too much thinking; some call it mindless TV. I really like comedies and found that watching funny shows and movies lifted my spirits and helped put my situations in perspective. I know this helped my overall mental and physical health. In order to stay positive, I stayed away from violent or sad programs.

11. A vacation can be as long as an hour. A vacation, or 'stay-cation', can be as simple as a picnic in a park, a walk with your dogs, volunteering, singing karaoke, having a night out with friends, date night with someone special, a date with special children in your life, just to name a few. If you are having

trouble thinking about what you can do, take a moment to think about what you love doing. Ask yourself a few questions to help determine your best options. What brings you peace? What helps you relax and unwind? What brings you passion or helps connect you with yourself? Then, schedule it, honor it, and do it. Remember, vacations can happen in any budget. If funds are tight, local museums or matinees are a great way to escape for a few hours.

12. I took my parents, at times, to the movies. Every time we did this, we would mumble going home that we wouldn't do that again. As their health allowed, and with both parents in wheelchairs, we would make the trek to the movie theater to get out of the house. It always seemed like a good idea at the time! There were times, though, when my dad couldn't make it to the bathroom and messed his pants. Other times, he would make a production out of complaining to whoever would listen about bathroom conditions. Sometimes, my dad needed to go to the bathroom more often than he was in the movie. My mom was another story. She peed her pants and needed twenty-minute bathroom trips during the movie. Even with an adult diaper, we found ourselves frequenting the bathroom more than the movie itself. Even leaving wasn't easy; it often took twenty minutes to get everyone back to the car. My parents enjoyed this time out and we balanced self with selfless giving. We would be sure to rotate and Felicity, Amanda, or Steven would alternate taking everyone to the movies. In the end, the movies brought us joy and a nice family outing.

13. I treated myself to massages once a month or every other month at a local massage center that had reasonable prices. Reasonable prices can be found everywhere from major chains to local massage schools. Many students provide these services at deeply discounted rates and they do a pretty good job.

14. I granted myself time alone and went to my bedroom and shut the door. In 2000, my parents left New Hampshire, where they planned on retiring, and moved to Arizona to help me though a significant life crisis. Back then, there were six of us (sometimes seven when Felicity visited) sharing a three-bedroom apartment. My parents shared a room, Amanda and Felicity shared a room and I shared a room with Sarah and Steven. Steven rotated among the rooms; whereas, Sarah was attached to my hip. This time around, I was fortunate with such a full house to have a room by myself with a door. With the exception of my mom needing to come through my room to use the restroom (before we got her a bedside potty), my family honored my closed door...most of the time. My dogs and cats, well, they don't care so much for closed doors. If you don't have a room with a door, you can go in your car; think of it as a mobile room. People don't typically think to look for you in the car!

15. I scheduled in my children's activities. Some were better than none. I attended Steven's football games, for example, and was so proud of him. I cheered him on and being there for him, for all of my kids' life events continue to this day as being one of my life's biggest rewards. Being available for my kids has been a priority for me. I was there for choir concerts, recitals, plays, and the like. I would not have had it any other way. If you have a special child in your life and they are involved with anything, I implore you to make it a priority to be there for them. They remember these times. It matters.

16. I asked for and received help, from dinner deliveries to prayers to rotating visits with my dad to basically any respite time off. My uncle Riley coming to visit gave me time to myself, and I appreciated this very much. Colleagues at work also offered to help when I found feeding my kids impossible when I was required to be at the hospital. Their helping with meals was a lifesaver to me and I have never forgotten their generosity and

compassion. At work one day in November 2009, before taking leave for abdominal surgery, an employee came into my office, sat at my desk, gave me a prayer cloth and asked if we could pray together. I was deeply touched. I accepted the prayer cloth and, as we prayed, I felt so blessed and supported. My staff meant everything to me and the outpouring of love and support was overwhelming at times—in a good way. If someone you know is going through a rough time, it only takes a minute to dial a phone or send a message letting that person know you are praying for them and are there if you need them. Being an independent woman and someone who didn't typically ask for or take people up on offers of help, I quickly realized I needed to learn to be a gracious receiver. When people offer to help, they generally mean it. ASK for help and watch as the support rolls in.

17. I cried. Crying is a great release. Typically I could hold it together publicly, but but as my head hit the pillow each night, I often grabbed my Kleenex and just cried my eyes out. I welcomed all the feelings I was experiencing—sadness, anger, fear, helplessness, anxiety - and embraced it as part of the process. Sometimes, I cried so loudly I found myself screaming, but I learned it's okay and to just let it out. I promise you will feel so much lighter for having done so.

Please know that all your feelings are completely normal. Sometimes you may be stuck with a particular emotion for a longer period than others, and other times you may quickly move through. When you feel angry, exhausted, loving, compassionate, frustrated and sad; sometimes within hours of each other, remember that there comes a time when, for your health, you must move from a place of being stuck or entrenched in the daily experience to release, allowing and acceptance. I recognize this is easier said than done. It takes time and integration of self-care tools to aid in releasing that which no longer serves you. Take deep breaths, relax and know everything you are feeling is normal.

18. I expressed gratitude for all the things I did have and that were going right in my life. When I found it difficult to see the good in my life, I had a bead necklace gratitude practice. As my fingers touched each bead, I would inwardly or outwardly state something I was grateful for and I forced myself to find enough topics to get through all the beads. Some days it was very tough finding things to be grateful for, but this is when gratitude is the most healing. Stick with it. Gratitude is one of the most powerful ways I know to bring more things into your life to be grateful for. If you have trouble finding things to be grateful for, start with little things like:

I am so grateful for eyes to see,
I am thankful for my ears to hear,
I give thanks for my hands to feel, write and hold things,
I am thankful for having clothes and a roof over my head,
I am so incredibly grateful for nature, music and water,
I am thankful for all my happy memories, and
I am grateful for each breath that I take.

"Gratitude makes sense of our past, brings peace for today, and creates a vision for tomorrow."
~ Melody Beattie

THINGS I COULD HAVE DONE BETTER AND PERSONAL ACTION GUIDE

"If you are headed in the wrong direction, God allows u-turns."
~ Author unknown

1. Exercise. I used to be an avid exerciser and exercised two to three house a day, five to six days a week. And I felt great! The last few years, however, I stopped exercising. The time to exercise is during periods of high stress, but I used the common

excuse I didn't have time and I paid the price. Exercising even fifteen minutes a day beyond the snippets of walking I did would have helped my mind and body. There are ways to exercise in all situations. One simple way to increase physical activity is to walk up and down stairs instead of taking elevators. Another idea is to park your car away from where you would normally park and get a few extra strides in as you walk to your destination.

2. Be as dedicated to my nutrition as I was my parents nutrition. I made too many visits to the Starbucks on the first floor of St. Joseph's Hospital. We would be too tired or get home too late to cook dinner and too often would stop for fast food. As I got through my third bout of cancer in mid 2011, I reaffirmed the connection between eating well and a health mind and body. I intellectually knew these things but I didn't practice it the last few years, and it showed. I was numb and going through the motions. More and more, I was eating to live, not living to eat. I am determined to get back to self and live the life I am meant to live. Had I embraced this philosophy a few years ago, I would have handled everything better, and this area for improvement would likely have been on the 'things I did well' list! I would have been a better caregiver because the family wouldn't have seen what a toll it took on me.

3. Maintain my weight. As a result of the above and eating my emotions, I gained over 60 pounds during the period of November 2009 and September 2010. That's an average of a five (5) pound gain a month! I believe everything happens for a reason and this is part of my journey. I share myself freely so it can help someone else avoid these mistakes. Five pounds easily creeps up on you and if not careful, a five-pound increase turns into 10 pounds, as so on. Think about the holidays where the average weight gain is around ten pounds. Now, imagine a year of holidays.

4. Write in a journal. Over the last nine years or so, I've intermittently written in journals. While I haven't journaled consistently, I found when I did write down my feelings, thoughts, and emotions, I released that which didn't serve me more easily. If I had it to do over again, I would have journaled daily. I did gratitude work in saying, thinking, or writing what I was thankful for everyday, yet didn't take time for daily journaling. I realize this may sound like a luxury when you are in the heart of a crisis, however, writing/journaling even 5 minutes a day supports the subconscious and provides a release.

5. Sleep. Sometimes I did this well and many times I did not. Good sleeping habits should be a way of life. I discussed this earlier in this chapter. I was better about this than I had been in previous years and could have taken this to an even greater level. I know better and will do better the rest of my life. One tip that helped me get a better rest was wearing eye masks. If you can, wear ear buds or get an ocean or rain forest CD to fall asleep. This helps keep noise levels down. These tips also apply when taking naps.

6. Internet. I could have limited my Internet usage time better. Perusing the web became an escape and incredible time waster; its amazing how one site leads to another and another and another. Can you relate to this? The Internet is important but, admittedly, I spent way too much time escaping and this kept me in a negative space. I quickly learned to limit my 'mindless internet surfing' to thirty minutes a day, and then stayed focused on things that mattered most. In addition is also bad for sleep. If you must read, read physical magazines or read good ol' fashion paper books and avoid e-reader books that produce light. The benefit of spending constructive down time is feeding yourself and your soul. I think technology is a main reason why families aren't spending enough time together.

7. No to Yes and Yes to No! Have you experienced the disease to please; the need to be liked, and do for others? I am better at honoring my wants, needs, goals and limitations. This means learning to say no to things that sound good but aren't part of my schedule. I learned the hard way that overbooking myself impacts my relationships, the quality of my work, overall well-being and self-esteem. I didn't realize the impact of this habit until some very important events and tasks were missed. More importantly, important relationships suffered. I felt out of integrity when I overcommitted and under delivered. I learned to prioritize and take smaller bites, so to speak, rather than try swallowing the entire elephant at once.

8. Activities. I would have made more time for activities I enjoy; such as dancing, ceramics, 1-on-1 days with my kids, or playing with my dogs.

9. Physical space and boundaries. I would have consistently honored my home space needs and habits. Prior to my parents moving in, everything had its place and my home was completely feng shui'd. I created an amazing living environment and the energy felt so great; my home was a peaceful sanctuary. But all of a sudden it was gone, and the reality was I allowed it to happen. I wrongly felt so bad for my parents and the changes they were going through that I didn't voice my own needs about not wanting to see their stuff spew into our dining room, kitchen, and my office areas. I misplaced sympathy and no one was happy. My sanctuary turned into a consolidated household with and everyone's stuff everywhere. The garage was no longer serving as a garage but yet another wall-to-wall storage space. Just like gaining 5 pounds at a time, this too can creep up on you and your household without ever realizing or noticing it. There are benefits to clearing 'stuff' out of a loved one's home prior to death. One benefit is you have the opportunity to share and learn the history of possessions, new or generational, and learn why it is important

to them. Then together you can make decisions whether to toss or keep, thereby eliminating any unnecessary confusion.

Never again will I allow someone else's way of living to interrupt my personal ebb and flow of positive energy I've worked so hard to create in my home. I remember one night Felicity telling me about how my mom declined Felicity's request to move the stuff on her table and work in the dining room. She said, "No, Tandy will get mad. I have to keep everything on my table." I felt relieved, and appreciated that my mom respected my needs and my point was now realized.

Half of this chapter was devoted to the self-care strategies I used to take care of myself and half of this chapter was devoted to things I could have done better. Self-care is vital and even more important when you assume the daunting task of caring for one or more loved ones. Getting enough rest, identifying and maintaining self-care routines, and taking time for yourself gives you the energy and capacity you need to fulfill your responsibilities. Make sure you identify your needs, speak your voice, and establish your ground rules immediately as a condition prior to involving yourself in a care giving role. If you put yourself first and take care of yourself you can and will effectively handle any situation.

"Nearly three quarters (72%) of family caregivers report not going to the doctor as often as they should and 55% say they skip doctor appointments for themselves. 63% of caregivers report having poor eating habits than non-caregivers and 58% indicate worse exercise habits than before caregiving responsibilities."[5]

~ National Alliance for Care giving and Evercare, 2006.

---

[5] *Evercare Study of Caregivers in Decline: A Close-Up Look at Health Risks of Caring for a Loved One. National Alliance for Caregiving and Evercare. 2006.*

CHAPTER SIX
Humor, Gratitude, and Compassion

"Never be afraid to laugh at yourself. After all, you could be missing out on the joke of the century."
~ Dame Edna Everage

Gratitude is the foundation for developing our greatness and is key to living a life filled with passion, peace and joy. It opens the door to endless abundance in all areas of life; attracting only that which serves our highest good.
~ Tandy Elisala

There are official definitions of humor, gratitude and compassion yet it is our relationships that really define it for us and bring it to life.

Humor

One of the best lessons my parents taught me was the importance of humor. Little did I know how much I needed this as an adult. Our entire family appreciates humor of all kinds. As such, we were able to recognize that humor was present in our lives starting the day of the accident. This first section of the chapter is dedicated to specific funny situations where we created more laughter since my dad's accident.

Humor is an incredibly powerful coping tool. We know, for it certainly helped us through many challenging times. What do you do when it's 6:00 A.M. and you've been up all night praying and your father wakes up for what would be a brief lucid time and ask where the coffee is? What do you do when it's 11:00 P.M. and your father has asked you at least twenty times where he is and why his head hurts? What do you do when, amid all this, your mother suddenly soils her clothes, her wheelchair, and the hospital floor? You both laugh. Then you laugh some more. Then you laugh so hard you cry! Laughing also helps minimize embarrassment about otherwise uncomfortable situations. Maybe it was a lack of sleep. Maybe we simply found humor in the situation. We learned to find humor in all situations. Laughter is medicine. Laughter is healing.

There were times, in between hospital stays, when my dad was at home and he thought it would be okay to parade around the house only wearing his underwear. When my kids had friends over to the house or my mom's home healthcare nurses visited, it made things a bit uncomfortable, but eventually one of us would inform our visitors that this was his new normal and not to worry because he won't remember anyone tomorrow. We'd all laugh; including my dad.

We laughed with my father when we visited him in the hospital. As we were cleaning out my parents' home, we found countless metal Folgers' coffee cans; you know, the large red cans with plastic tops. We counted so many of these cans and they were all empty. We scratched our heads in amazement, wondering what possessed him to save all these cans? One afternoon as we sat around his hospital bed talking about some of our discoveries at the house, Felicity said, "Well Dad, you said you wanted to be cremated. We can save money and use these coffee containers as urns. We could even decorate them." He chuckled, and then we laughed so hard we cried.

One day I was discussing the pros and cons of his upcoming brain surgery and one of us said, "Oh, why not, then he can parade around outside in his underwear. Maybe the dogs can take him for a walk with his black socks and white underwear!" Again we laughed. Granted, our humor may not be someone else's humor, but that's OK. I'm sure the nurses thought we were odd at times but we didn't care. Humor is a natural coping mechanism and a powerful healing agent and always puts things into perspective.

So, here we were with a wanderer in underwear and thoughts of being in England. Maybe we should have bought underwear from England and he could parade around in a Union Jack. When he wasn't in England or being the King of England, he thought he was in Texas, Washington D.C., or even California, before going back to being King of England all over again. It was so much fun listening to my father give my kids all kinds of titles. Humor not only heals but also grants us amazing, cherished memories. One day my dad wondered why the local TV referenced Arizona but nothing about England. He had a very logical and reasonable explanation for everything. Humor runs in the family. This accident made national news and while watching scenes from the accident on TV, my uncle Riley, noting a large man in black socks being put in a helicopter, exclaimed, "That is my brother. I'd know his belt line and black socks anywhere!"

Gratitude

> *Gratitude unlocks the fullness of life. It turns what we have into enough, and more. It turns denial into acceptance, anger to peace, chaos to order, hopelessness to hope and confusion to clarity.*
>
> *~ adapted from Melodie Beattie*

Every experience has the power we give it. Being in a state of gratitude is one of my core values. I have always integrated gratitude into my everyday life. This is one of the best ways I know of keeping my balance and perspective.

> *"Gratitude is not only the greatest of virtues, but the parent of all the others."*
>
> *~ Cicero*

Many of us understand the word gratitude. Our parents taught us to say 'please' and 'thank you' at the appropriate times. Growing up, my mother imparted the very important lesson of writing thank you cards and notes to people who sent cards and gifts. Gratitude can be defined as a feeling of thankfulness or appreciation. The essence of gratitude is found in all things; big and small. I believe we all need to find things to be grateful for, everyday, through good times and in bad. There are countless blessings I found through my care giving experience and ways I saw gratitude demonstrated in others.

The more we are thankful the more things we have to be thankful for in our lives. I learned that when we take life too seriously, the stress in doing so causes our bodies to physically ache. Gratitude and humor go hand in hand.

Gratitude is a state of being; it's really a way of life. For example, I mentioned there was a time when Felicity was living with us. It was during Felicity's period of having a suspended driver's license; she lived with us. She has an allergic sensitivity to dogs, but she also knew my dogs weren't going anywhere; in fact, they weren't going anywhere for dad or for anyone. She walked around with puffy eyes and a red nose for nearly a month and did not complain once. She was grateful to have all of our support, and we were grateful she was alive and making huge strides to overcome her addiction.

Some mornings when I took Felicity to work, I was half dressed and would go outside without my top buttoned or my hair looking like I put my finger in an electric socket. What people didn't know was how much effort I took to look that good on those days! In reality, I was thankful to simply make it out of bed. Some days, my mom and I both wore our pajamas to the doctor's office for blood work or treatments. We were thankful to have medical insurance. We were thankful for waterless shampoo when showers were a luxury. We were thankful for a dependable car when driving close to two hours a day for my mom's radiation treatments. I got frustrated at times with my dad for asking the same thing over and over, yet I'm so thankful for I had the extra time with him and he didn't die in the car accident. I quickly got tired of long twenty-minute treks to the car with my parents, yet I was thankful for the slower pace because it forced me to deepen my appreciation for nature. In sum, during this time, I started a new habit everyone in the house came to recognize and laugh about. When I got home from wherever it was, changed, and took off my bra, I was done. No bra means I'm not going anywhere the rest of the day. Period. Now, my family doesn't bother asking me to go anywhere when my bra is off. It isn't happening!

I learned that when I really reached for little things to be grateful for, like a doctor having the right words to say or the right nurse being on call or a bed opening up when needed, more amazing things happened in my life and just at the right times.

"Gratitude makes sense of our past, brings peace for today, and creates a vision for tomorrow."

            ~ Melody Beattie

Compassion

Many have heard the saying, "charity begins at home." I believe this to be true and would also add so does compassion. Compassion takes many forms. It can mean releasing judgments about people; such as the resentment and negative feelings I had about my parents neglecting their health over the years. "The golden years aren't so golden," some say. Others say, "If I would have known I was going to live so long, I would have taken better care of myself." Compassion can mean learning incredible patience with your parents when they ask the same thing twenty times a day or forget to relay important information to someone. Compassion can mean forgiveness, and in my case, forgiving my father for moving us my second semester of my senior year in high school, and forgiving myself for unhealthy eating habits and a second failed marriage.

I found making decisions with a compassionate heart brought peace with decisions I made and was vital for my healing and all my relationships. Experiencing my dad's declining health firsthand with every surgery and complication and experiencing the bond and closeness of our family, integrating humor was an effective release.

With all my emotions surrounding my parent's health, I looked inward and took inventory of my own health. I realized I was angry with and at myself for allowing myself to neglect my own physical and mental health. My weight gain and many bad decisions came rushing through my head like a ferris wheel; going round and round ever so slowly with periodic stops to ponder the scenes from my life. I realized that I didn't want my kids to ever, ever feel about me the way I felt about my parents. I realized I needed to be well for me and my future and the peace I have knowing I am healthy, fit and well. With this realization, I was able to change my relationship with food. Being with feelings isn't the same as drowning in them. The truth is it's never about the food; it's about what's above, below, in-between, in front of and in back of our feelings.

This experience also helped me realize what I look for in relationships. I want to be in a relationship where my future boyfriend or husband takes proper care of himself. I realize this isn't a guarantee of perfect health but it sure helps! I also realized that I needed to BE the person I wanted to attract. Like attracts like. When we are grateful for what we have, we attract more of what we already have and what we want into our lives.

An example of compassion in action occurred one night the end of January 2010. Feeling overwhelmed never seemed to end. This night would be no different. As our family was together celebrating my mom being in remission, Felicity was involved in another car accident. Amanda showed her wings through her immense compassion to and for Felicity. Given the severity of the situation and my mounting anger with Felicity over a series of events before this happened, Amanda drove and my dad came along for the ride to pick her up...at the police station. Nonetheless, he understandably wanted to see his baby girl.

Little did we know Felicity's personal struggles from the last several months caught up with her in the form of dependency on medications for her physical recovery, depression, and anxiety. None of us had ever experienced an addiction to prescription drugs and we didn't know the signs. Felicity knew I was furious with her and she would have rather gone to jail than come home with us that night. She could see the seething anger in my eyes and my head pulsing from my blood pressure rising. At one point, she turned to the police officers and, I learned later, almost said, "No, take me to jail. I don't want to go home with my sissy."

Felicity fell right into my arms and she started crying and apologizing over and over. I rubbed her back and told her everything would be okay, yet right now I was angry and disappointed. Immediately thereafter, Amanda put her arm around Felicity and put her in the back seat furthest from me. Our dad sat with Felicity in the back seat while I screamed, yelled, and lectured on the way home. I was crying out of anger and sadness. I was shaking out of rage and disappointment. Meanwhile, my dad repeatedly whispered to Felicity, with no recollection of why we were even there, that he wasn't sure why I was so upset. He was showing immense compassion towards his baby girl. Between her tears and hyperventilating, she explained being in a car accident and arrested for driving under the influence of prescription medication may have a factor with her emotions and my rants! Our dad's reply was, "It's okay, at least you are alive." I was so angry at the time that, to me, it was obvious she was alive and I could skip this and go straight into lecture mode. His response is probably exactly what Felicity needed to hear from him in that moment and was probably one of his most compassionate expressions of love.

After about an hour of yelling, I calmed down and told Felicity I loved her and I was glad she was okay. Cars can be replaced but she can't. When Amanda drove Felicity home later that night, again demonstrating her immense compassionate heart, my mom sat at the edge of the bed and starting crying. As tears streamed down her face, I sat next to her and put my arm around her. My head touching hers, we both cried. We cried because we were sad, disappointed, and scared. What would happen to Felicity? Would she spend time in jail because of this? Would the people she hit be okay? How would she pay any financial obligations as a result of all this? Surely, her license would be suspended for a period of time. How would Felicity get to work and home? She lives in a rural town that doesn't even have home mail delivery or city bus routes, and if she didn't work, she couldn't support herself. How badly was she addicted to medications? Would she need in-patient treatment? What could we do to support her? At what point could we trust Felicity again?

At the end of the day, we knew family was family. We would be there for each other no matter what. My mom and I then did what any responsible family member would do: hide all pain and other medications with addicting properties. I rounded up all bottles and put them in a locking safe. My mom and I had the only keys and nobody else in the house knew what we did. I was sad that we felt we had to do this, particularly since my mom was still on pain medication from cancer surgery, various foot and ankle breaks, sprains and cellulites infections so pain medication required extra planning. If this extra step would prevent Felicity from accessing any of our medications, then that's what we were going to do.

As you can probably gather by now, Amanda is wise beyond her years. Amanda being there for her Aunt in such a compassionate, patient and loving way was yet another example of Amanda's character. This is just one of the countless ways Amanda modeled compassion. To give you a larger sense of who Amanda is, with her permission, I'm sharing one of her class assignments:

"The most important thing I can do is make someone feel like they matter, that I won't forget them and that they had a purpose." As Elie Wiesel put it in his Nobel Peace Speech, "…these victims need above all is to know that they are not alone; that we are not forgetting them…that while their freedom depends on ours, the quality of our freedom depends on theirs." Very often in aide work, you rarely forget the faces of the people you meet – the ones who you work for, who don't have voices to speak for themselves.

In a world with over six billion people on it, with economies that dwarf that number and resources to solve problems – there is no excuse for anyone to be victims of circumstance. Social justice and human right issues speak to me the most, so by getting a degree in Global Health, I am creating a lifelong commitment to my family, community, and to the world in that with pursuing rights for all, I am also contributing to a responsibility chain.

In the book, *The Last Lecture,* Randy Pausch writes about being a communitarian, the connection between the individual and community – that when we connect with others, we become better people. It is only through that belief that I have a responsibility to others to do what I can, when I can, with what I have and there is nothing shameful in that."

Amanda Elisala

I truly feel this entire journey has given me more patience, compassion, and love. I felt my parents were my master teachers throughout my care giving journey. They taught me so many life principles, and yet I don't think they realized just how much I learned from them. I am so eternally grateful for placing a higher value on humor. Two years ago, I probably wouldn't have been able to laugh at myself as comfortably as I do now. I've learned that if you can't laugh at yourself, you are taking life way too seriously. I mentioned in an earlier chapter that I learned so much patience as a result of my parent's respective health conditions. It's taken the patience of Job to a whole other level for me. I found comfort in scripture; especially the Story of Job, which I remember from my childhood.

These experiences and lessons learned definitely helped and manifested in greater closeness with my kids. We were close before my father's accident, but our entire family has grown even closer. Having the bond of our experiences with my mom and dad and our humor and love for one another has enriched our lives so fully that others also seem to notice our authentic love. As my parents' health deteriorated and times seemed unbearable, I didn't know my compassion was blossoming into a garden of grace. People say when one door closes another opens. I just didn't realize the door would be the doorway to my heart and soul.

KEY LESSONS LEARNED

1. *Find humor and laughter in your everyday life and situations will automatically be lighter and more manageable.* Share your experiences with others and laugh together in the humor. Laughter is great medicine. We laughed so much we could have had our own reality show. I guarantee everyone watching would have had many belly laughs.

2. Realizing that 'good is good enough' is exactly what you need sometimes. Everything doesn't have to be perfect. Good enough is okay most of the time.

3. Be patient. Have faith. Realizing you aren't going to change or control situations outside of your direct control can help you develop the patience you need to get through most situations. Everything will work out as intended. Evoke your reservoir of patience and compassion when working with loved ones who

need extra assistance or time to do things; they will be grateful and you will be happier.

4. A prayer that has always resonated with me the prayer of St. Francis of Assisi (1181-1226), which so poetically sums everything up:

    "Lord, make me an instrument of your peace;
    where there is hatred, let me sow love;
    when there is injury, pardon;
    where there is doubt, faith;
    where there is despair, hope;
    where there is darkness, light;
    and where there is sadness, joy.
    Grant that I may not so much seek
    to be consoled as to console;
    to be understood, as to understand,
    to be loved as to love;
    for it is in giving that we receive,
    it is in pardoning that we are pardoned,
    and it is in dying [to ourselves] that we are born to eternal life."
    — St. Francis of Assisi

FAMILY ACTION GUIDE

1. Demonstrate compassion for yourself. Your physical, mental, emotional, and spiritual self need support and loving care.

2. Bring even more laughter in your everyday life. Listen to funny music, watch funny movies or funny Utube videos. There certainly isn't a lack of content! These are great ways to bring more laughter in your everyday life.

3. Have a a consistent verbal gratitude practice among all family members present in the house or hospital. Go around the room

and tell each other things you are grateful for in that moment builds a higher level of energy and positivity.

4. Demonstrate more compassion for yourself. Your physical, mental, emotional, and spiritual self need support and loving care. Your eyes aren't deceiving you, I purposely listed this as the first and last part of this chapter's action guide because it is so important.

5. One final note. When talking about humor, gratitude and compassion, I wanted to share some specific, practical tips you can use to effectively manage stress. Stress prevents us from being in our natural state of perfection. Below are some stress management tips and thoughts about anger:

    a. Several times a day, take five (5) deep breaths, breathing in through the nose and out through the mouth. Visualizing positive things on the in-breath and letting go of stress, negativity, illness on the out breath is a proven technique to reduce stress and instantly bring calm. I can attest, this really helps me cope and center myself during the good times and bad. I recommend doing this several times a day for your overall well being. To take it a step further, you can imagine a plus [+] sign on the in breath and a minus [-] sign on the out breath. Think about your 'story', who you share it with and what purpose it serves. I should have minimized the number of times I told my "story" about my parents and our lives in general. You see, what we focus on persists. Is it a surprise then that my engaging in negative 'stories' about the goings on in our family created more stress and disease in my life? In hindsight, no. There were a lot of loving people who were there to listen and asked how we were all coping, but I could have responded differently. We all have a story and can be attached to it. Had I refrained from "going there," so to speak, I think all the positive things I was doing would have worked that much better for everyone.

6. Think before you speak. Sometimes, we can get caught up in our drama and trauma that we want to share all the gory, negative details; whether it's a funny story or a serious one. Here are some questions you can ask yourself before chomping at the bit to tell a story.

   a. Is this an appropriate story to share?
   b. Is this the right place and time to tell the story?
   c. How is it relevant, what energy would it bring, and how will it benefit others?
   d. Am I the right person to tell the story?

7. When I was angry with others, I eventually remembered to hold up a mirror and ask myself what part of me is angry with myself. What part of me keeps things in my home that no longer serve me? What part of me is addicted (in my case, addicted to food)? What part of me feels out of control? Ask yourself these questions and you will gain tremendous insight.

Taking the time to reassess why you get angry in any situation and who you are angry with can get muddled. Understanding the underlying purpose of the anger, how this anger manifests in your life, and expressing anger in an appropriate way and the right time is indeed difficult, at best. Holding onto anger only hurts ourselves; it doesn't hurt the person or the subject. Don't let people live in your head rent-free, release the anger and focus on bringing out the best in you and your life.

The more gratitude you feel and express, really feel; the more your thoughts really do help create your future. Make sure your thoughts serve you and all involved for the greater good. Remember, the more gratitude you have and share, the more the universe conspires to bring into your life even more things for which to be grateful. May we all recognize and feel the importance of being in a state of gratitude, how to capitalize on humor in difficult situations, and the healing power of compassion.

"Your thoughts and beliefs of the past have created this moment, and all the moments up to this moment. What you are now choosing to believe and think and say will create the next moment and the next day and the next month and the next year."

~ Louise Hay

CHAPTER SEVEN
The Power of a Support System

"I've learned that people will forget what you said, people will forget what you did, but people will never forget how you made them feel."

~ *Maya Angelou*

A s is true for a lot of people, I have gone through many tough times in my life. One thing I know I can always count on is my support system. The unconditional love that comes with this support helped me get through the darkest hour. The hour-long talks with Felicity at 10:00 pm in front of a gas station were priceless. One night, we sat in front of the gas station in the car for so long just venting, laughing, talking, and laughing some more, and, before long, we realized we witnessed a robbery. Speaking of cars, Felicity laughed at me when she came over to the house and saw me simply sitting in my car alone, enjoying the solitude. It was times like these that released stress, helped us stay connected and help us know we are not alone.

An ice cream run with a neighbor, dinners with friends, food colleagues dropped off when I didn't have time to feed my growing kids, prayer cloths and prayers, and supportive text messages were some examples of the many types of support I received and learned to graciously accept. At times, the smallest act of support was actually the biggest moment of my day.

The day I resigned from my twenty-one-year career, I received hundreds of emails in the days, weeks and months to come, I received even more positive thoughts and offers of help. Aunt Tandy and Uncle Riley visited a few times between December 2009-June 2010, and this helped me remember I had others I could rely on. They provided comfort, love, and support when I needed it.

During one of my dad's hospital stays in October/November 2010, Stacey and her husband, Anthony, unexpectedly came to the hospital to pray with and for my dad. They gave him a prayer cloth and visited with him for a while. This gesture really touched my heart and it certainly made a lasting impact with my dad. My dad was never one to go to church or pray publically, but like most people he had deeper beliefs and a personal relationship with God. Even when he forgot they visited, he held the cloth they gave him and would tell me, "Some of your friends from work gave this to me. They were very nice people." Another friend and colleague, Anna, helped me by sharing her experience of caring for a loved one with a traumatic brain injury and offered several tips that I incorporated into our lives. Talking to someone who had been there was extremely comforting and I realized I was not alone.

The benefits person I worked with at my dad's employer was truly amazing. Ironically, Laura and I knew each other through a fraternal youth organization we were both members of growing up. Little did I know she would be the person I needed to worked with to help navigate my father's confusing medical leave, extended leave, and benefits program. Laura worked tirelessly and proactively to take care of things for my parents, keeping a watchful eye for anything I needed to do or be informed about; even to the point of assisting me when she was on vacation with her family. Another great support was my dad's manager, Jim. Jim sent cards from his department, notified me of impending paperwork deadlines, and called periodically to check on my dad.

My parent's used to frequent Macayo's Mexican Restaurant in Casa Grande. Sandy was their mainstay waitress. She got to know my parents over the years, expressed concern about my dad's condition and several times, offered to help our family with the gift of food. We took her up on this offer and she delivered a huge, delicious, and filling platter full of food. It was such a sweet gesture and we appreciated her thoughtfulness and the time it took her to bring this to us. This food hit the spot.

Connecting with others is critical for our continued emotional growth and development. While there is no substitute for personal face-to-face connections, social media; facebook in particular, has grown to be a positive, useful tool for me. Through all the family ups and downs, I found Facebook to be a huge time saver by posting family updates instead of having to make additional daily calls. One message and, waa laa, everyone saw updates about my parents. Of course, when things were grim and we thought we were losing my dad, I reached out and called close family members personally. I so appreciated getting to know my extended family more through these trials and tribulations. The 'thinking of you,' 'praying for you all,' 'hang in there,' and related messages helped immensely. This support has meant the world to us. We have a strong yearning now to learn more about our family history as a result of these meaningful connections and their support. Felicity and Amanda have since dug out our various family genealogy research and work on Ancestry.com to fill in the blanks.

Our extended family has annual reunions and typically rotates the location between east and west coasts. As result of my parents' declining health, the family made the unprecedented decision to change the reunion dates AND came to Arizona in the middle of July just so we could participate. This meant a great deal to my family and was another example of incredible support.

Some people we meet in life touch our hearts and lives profoundly. Such as the case with my dear friend, Tanna. Tanna always helped me put any situation in perspective and always looked out for my best interest, both personally and professionally. She also knew just the right thing to say at just the right time. She intuitively gave me cards when I needed them most, visited my family, and helped me see the forest from the trees when it was difficult for me to see even myself at times. She left me uplifting voice messages, took me to the movies, and brought me Jamba Juice[6] when I couldn't eat solid foods after my own surgeries. We laughed together. We cried together. She has taught me so much and our friendship made these tough times seem bearable. I certainly wouldn't have handled my own healing as well as I did without her love, support, and encouragement. Trust and friendship is believing in and knowing each others' weaknesses and loving each other anyway.

---

[6] Smoothie drink restaurant

When I was diagnosed with cancer the first and second time, one of my previous bosses, John, who had left the organization we worked for to serve as CEO for another company, called me. John told me he had heard about my cancer surgery and wanted me to know he and his family were praying for me. He let me know "We are all here for you" and told me to let him know if I needed anything. This simple gesture made a huge and lasting impact on me. This is a man I would move mountains for and thankfully had the opportunity to work for him again. It meant a lot to me that John cared enough about me as a person, to reach out to me. I am fortunate to have had some bosses in my life that, I felt, really truly cared for me and others around them.

Such is the case with my long-time boss and mentor, Nina, who also kept in touch. She sent flowers and called several times to check on me and see how everyone was doing, and her encouragement kept me feeling positive about things. We went to lunch periodically (not enough!) to catch up. We worked together for about 20 years, and I feel so fortunate to have such a caring example of leadership with such a talented and compassionate woman. She was the best person I have ever had the honor and privilege of working for and with.

My dogs provided unconditional love and support during this time as did my cat, Emma. When I was particularly sad or feeling less than 100 percent, Emma would curl up on my bed next to my head and start purring loudly. I found this so healing and comforting. She stayed that way all night at times. My dogs, Roxy and Colonel, always knew when I was sad or when any of us in the house needed them. One day, after a particularly hard day at work, I plopped on the recliner and started crying. Roxy jumped on my lap and started licking my tears away. This gesture made me cry more because I was so thankful for her! Roxy would provide immense support for my dad and saved both my parents' lives on more than one occasion. I truly believe she came into our lives a year before all of this happened to help us through these hard times. Had I known how amazing dogs were for us humans, I would have had dogs decades ago. I can tell you this—I will always have at least one dog around me the rest of my life.

Several of Felicity's friends were absolutely amazing support for our family. They were so good for Felicity and added humor to her life. On several occasions, these amazing friends, Amanda and Mary, brought several days worth of food to our house. They played games with Felicity, watched movies and laughed. The laughter and positive energy was a great pick me up for our house at the time. They reached out to us on multiple occasions, offering support, prayers, and counsel.

During Felicity's darkest hour, I reached out to Amanda and Mary for help. They rose to the occasion, reached out to Felicity when she needed them most. Being able to reach out to them and ask for their help was probably the only way Felicity would have had the support she needed from friends whom she feared would judge her for her addiction. Quite the opposite occurred; they listened with an open heart and supported her during this difficult time. It is important to remember that addiction is emotional, not logical. While sometimes tough love is needed, having understanding, supportive, and nonjudgmental people around us, can be just as, if not, a more powerful support system. Families at the preschool Felicity worked at also offered support and understanding. The owner even paid for Felicity's doctors' appointments so she could take care of her health and heal.

"The friend who can be silent with us in a moment of despair or confusion, who can stay with us in an hour of grief and bereavement, who can tolerate not knowing...not healing, not curing...that is a friend who cares."
~ Henri Nouwen

Here I was a single mom to kids and pets, daughter caregiver extraordinaire, cancer survivor, and knee-deep in a fraternal youth organization (Job's Daughters), as an elected advisor. I felt so guilty that I couldn't fulfill my previously committed obligations, as my parents were now my first priority. I felt like such a terrible mom for not being there for Sarah at this pivotal point in her life. Amanda had been there and done it many times over and just picked it up and made it happen. Once again, I felt immense gratitude and unconditional love for and from Amanda and Sarah. Sarah understood why I simply couldn't help her. This ceremony is like planning a mini wedding; it's a huge event. Our family's involvement in Job's Daughters goes back several generations. A few times when the girls were discussing the upcoming events, I cried because I felt a deep ache in my heart for not being present when Sarah needed my support and guidance. No amount of reassurance from them took the ache away. All I did at that point was pray my parents' health condition remained stable through Sarah's installation. For us, it was Job's Daughters. This could also apply to Eagle Scout ceremonies, significant girl scout milestone ceremonies or other related event.

As quickly as things seemed to become somewhat manageable, the perfect storm occurred. One evening in early May 2011, my daughter, Sarah, was being installed (sworn in) as the presiding officer for Job's Daughters International. Because of my parent's needs, Amanda and Sarah planned the ceremony and Sarah's entire term of office activities, fundraisers, and charity by themselves, when typically, it is a family affair. I really struggled inside, like a tug of war, balancing all areas in my life. Like a juggler with eight balls in the air, I felt like they all could fall to the ground at any moment. I was fragile and the balls in the air felt like glass and everything could come crumbling down around me. Every step I took felt like sharp glass.

At this stage, my mom was back home recovering from a hospital stay and my dad was in his third stint at a rehabilitation center and had been there thirty-six hours when I got a call. There is a saying that *you never know how strong you are until being strong is the only choice you have available to you.* I couldn't have said it any better. On a beautiful Friday morning, as I loaded our car with boxes of things for Sarah's big evening, my dad's rehabilitation center called. His blood sugar was under forty and he was nonresponsive. My dad had gone into cardiac arrest and was intubated with a machine breathing for him. He was in the ambulance en route to the hospital. The rehabilitation center told me it didn't look good and the hospital needed me there immediately.

Seriously, I thought. Really? Now of all days!?! I always felt that God didn't give us more than we could handle, but now I was wavering from this philosophy, at least for a few moments. I rushed inside, told my mom what was happening, and she set the a new speed record for getting ready. It's important to note that my mom's idea of 'rushing to get ready' was a minimum of thirty minutes. I told her I needed to get to the hospital NOW. She was in her wheelchair ready with her oxygen and purse in hand by the front door in no time.

When we arrived at the hospital, the doctor said the only thing his team could do was help my dad be comfortable. He wasn't responding to sugar IV's to raise his blood sugar or other medical interventions. It seemed everything they did to help one problem negatively impacted another part of his body. His organs were finally shutting down, permanently. Hours went by and he was still unable to breathe on his own. The doctors now advised us to let family know if they wanted to see him, now was the time. Then, the nurses gave us hospice information. I called Aunt Tandy and Uncle Riley immediately and told them the situation.

I took my mom to the bathroom and we sat there in silence, pondering the reality of the situation. As I took several deep breaths with my hands on my heart, I suddenly felt like a ton of bricks was on my chest and I struggled to take breaths. When I looked up I saw several tears roll down my mom's face. She tried to wipe away the tears and suppress her emotions, but we were both realizing what was happening to dad. Neither one of us needed to or could say much in that moment. I tried to reassure her that everything would be okay. We've been through this before with such a roller coaster of emotions and waves of events that would test the strongest of families. We both felt the wave of sadness, anxiety, peace, relief, anger, and stress in that moment, yet felt we both needed to be strong—for the family and for each other. We both wiped our respective tears and I helped her back to his room.

As quickly as these tender emotional moments came, they were replaced by the hustle and bustle of ER activity. My dad still declining, doctors found a new brain bleed; complicating the situation. He had been through so much and consistently declined after each brain surgery. My mom, Felicity, and I previously decided we weren't allowing any more brain surgeries so now we had to decide whether we were going to stick by this difficult decision. After discussing it, we decided to have him transported back to Barrow.

I felt a peaceful feeling that the end was close and, as sad as it was, we would be able to return to a somewhat normal life. I felt taking care of my mom would be a walk in the park compared to taking care of my dad. Her limitations were of a physical nature, whereas his were of a neurological and physical nature. Traumatic Brain Injuries (TBI) can be taxing on all involved. Like it or not. Fair or not. Right or not. This is how I felt.

I was now faced with the decision of staying with my parents at the hospital or leaving and supporting Sarah that evening. I knew that if my dad died while I was gone, he would have wanted me to be with Sarah. Felicity quickly relieved me, spent time with our dad, and took care of my mom while I drove across town to be with Sarah. A few miles away from the ceremony location, a fellow adult advisor, Matt, called my cell phone and whispered, "Tandy, your daughter is being caped and crowned." He held the phone up so I could hear what was going on. I started crying, cursing and couldn't believe after all of this, I would miss this special, once in a lifetime moment. By the grace of God, I arrived literally just in time to see my beautiful daughter being crowned (a highlight of the ceremony). I breathed a sigh of relief and gave thanks that everyone helped ensure I made it to see this blessed event. I later learned that everyone tried delaying the ceremony as long as possible until I got there. They started late and they spoke slowly throughout the evening until I could arrive.

If only my support system could turn my dad's deteriorating health around. Shortly after the ceremony, I returned to Barrow's. Felicity and I rotated being with our dad. This was it—the end. So many emotions were swirling around in my body. I felt dizzy. I was thankful we were there for each other and shuttered at what would happen next.

KEY LESSONS LEARNED

1. *First and foremost, we ALL need a support system.* Whether it's family, friends, volunteer organizations, church, colleagues, mentors, sororities, fraternities, support groups relate to what you and/or family are going through during a time of need.

Whoever it is, reach out, embrace, and accept your support system. Initially, we didn't want to burden others, but true friends want to help. Friends wanting to bring dinner for the family. Bring it. Family offering to come and help clear out homes and storage units. Please do. Family and friends offering to take my kids places, yes, thank you. Families offering to take care of my parents for a few hours while I rest, go see a movie, or do whatever I needed to do at that time. Thank you. Friends visiting to offer prayer and comfort. You betcha. These are powerful ways our support system rose to the occasion.

"We all have the power to create the life we really want to have. The key is finding the tools and support system that will help us to most easily and quickly bring forth, from within, our highest and best."

                                                    ~ Author unknown

2. People who say they want to help are not always there when you finally do ask for help. I quickly learned which friends just wanted to be there for the fun times and which friends would be there in the middle of the night. There is a saying that if someone can't handle me during my worst times they certainly don't deserve me during the good ones. This sums up real friends.

3. Allow others to help! Just as we like to help in a time of need we need to allow others that service to themselves. When we reject offers of help, we are rejecting a part of ourselves. We also take away from the gifts others want to give us.

Remember, "For it is in giving that we receive."
                                                    ~ St. Francis of Assisi

4. Strength. To be in need is not the same as being weak. Being weak is not asking for help. Accepting and asking for help demonstrates our strength and self love.

5. I wish I would have found a way to attend church regularly. While I'm not a particularly religious person, I am extremely spiritual. I find it comforting to be in the presence of like-minded people and just be in silence. Bottom line here is I should have supported myself on all levels more proactively.

6. I should have had at least one night a week where our family (whoever wasn't in a hospital) consistently ate together at the dinner table. This would have helped us stay even more connected.

"A wife's hospitalization increased her husband's chances of dying within a month by 35%. A husband's hospitalization boosted his wife's mortality risk by 44%."[7]

7. As the above quote indicates, when one spouse is hospitalized, it significantly impacts the other spouse in profound ways. Aside from the obvious physical and emotional health impacts, there can be other impacts to a marriage. The second my dad has his accident, my mother lost companionship; including their sexual relationship. As uncomfortable as this topic may be, the reality is when one spouse either watches or actively participates in the others' care, their relationship changes. My mom didn't have any friends she could talk to about her marriage; her innermost fears and feelings about this part of their relationship changing. I felt like I wanted to take her somewhere to make friends so she could have an outlet.

I realized the significance of this lack of support my mom felt when one day she quietly said to me, "Tandy, I don't have any

---

[7] Nicholas D. Christakis, Professor, Health-care Policy, Harvard Medical School, Boston and Suzanne Salamon, M.D., Associate Chief, Geriatric Psychiatry, Beth Israel Deaconess Hospital, Boston, New England Journal of Medicine, Feb. 16, 2006

friends to talk to and I need to talk so I'm going to talk to you." She got my attention.

FAMILY ACTION GUIDE

1. Some people find their support groups through places of worship. However your support system shows up for you, proactively seek it out. This could include taking advantage of hospital support groups.

2. Allow others to help. Sometimes, it's difficult for us to receive. Now is the time to let the grace of God come through.

3. Thank those that help you along the way.

4. If you are caring for your spouse, you need someone to talk to outside the home and other family members. I was okay having a conversation with my mother about her lack of physical intimacy with my dad but this may not be appropriate in all situations. I doubt my mom was 'glad' to share this with me and she probably would have preferred talking to a friend or counselor. If you are caring for an elder; such as a parent or grandparent, recognize they may need to talk to someone outside the home about how to cope with their changing relationship. The same holds true for spouses caring for each other.

Remember, "No matter what happens, or how bad it seems today, life does go on, and it will be better tomorrow."
~ Maya Angelou

CHAPTER EIGHT
Balancing Independence and Safety

"The recognition of the existence of a problem is the first step in its solution."

~ Martin H. Fischer

There are practical daily life activities that caregivers and their loved ones face every day. How we handle these situations determines the extent of healing and the respect and dignity your loved ones experience. We need to know when to sit back and let them be and when to step in and help. We must hone our communication skills to effectively manage situations that arise with conflict. In my case, our communication strategies required significant shifts with my dad as a result of his TBI. There is a difference between care giving and care taking. Often, we think by doing things for our loved ones we are helping them. In reality, the very thing we think is helping them actually serves to create sadness, inferiority, anger, hostility, and adversely affect their well-being. In sum, it can have a reverse effect and take away what little independence they may have left.

We need to be prepared with the right tools to handle these situations to avoid hurting our loved ones emotionally. Whether practical matters involve the home or communication with family and friends, understanding where your loved one is coming from can help you promote a sense of independence and dignity. They will respect you and they will respect themselves. Let's explore some specific examples of that fine line between care giving and care taking.

As you have gathered thus far, the consequences of brain injuries or other illnesses are unpredictable. In total, my dad had multiple surgeries, seizures, a brain infection, several blood clots and TIA's, (mini-strokes), just to name a few. He suffered continual short-term memory loss, cognitive deterioration, and lost full use of his right arm.

The brain is a complex organ. I had no previous experience with brain injuries and it took time, mistakes, trial and error, observation, intuition, and research to learn how to best provide us a safe environment.

My dad was a proud man. He rarely asked for help and always took care of those in need. He became frustrated with himself for not being able to do things he used to be able to do or talk the way he used to talk or remember things that came easily for him to remember. I watched him evolve from being a good patient early on in his recovery to being an agitated, hostile, angry, and stubborn man.

At first, I wanted to jump and do things to make things easier for him. While I think I had a good gauge on his limitations, I think we all misread his abilities at first and did things for him without giving him a chance to try doing for himself. Eventually, I learned to relax more and specifically do things for him unless he asked which usually happened after he tried something repeatedly, got fed up and gave up. The exception to this hands-off rule was when he learned to walk with a walker. He was so unstable that someone always had a grip on the back of his shirt, his arm, or with a gait belt around his waist. This strategy and intuitive knowing saved him from falling countless times.

I felt so sad seeing my dad this way. As a side note, prior to the accident, he was in a doctoral degree program. He valued education and was a lifelong learner. Never one with a shortage of books, CD's, tapes, periodicals or magazines to keep his mind sharp, we wondered whether he would ever be able to read again, much less return to school and obtain his doctorate degree. I remember feeling so proud when he asked me one day whether I knew why he chose the University of Phoenix to pursue his master's and doctoral degree programs. When I replied that I did not know, he said that he wanted to get a degree from the school I was the Registrar for and get a transcript with my name on it. I was Registrar for this school at that time and my chest boasted with pride when he made this comment. It was then I realized he was truly proud of me. What a moment I'll never forget.

As my dad healed, he started reading his collection of Tom Clancy, Alex Haley, James Patterson, and Dan Brown books and I noticed that he would stay on the same page day after day, week after week. Eventually, he started forming new memories and was able to get through multiple pages a day. Then, he got to a point where he read the same book sometimes two, three, or four times before moving on to another book. He reread the same book to compare what he retained from the time before. Pretty good recall strategy if you ask me!

My dad loved helping people and talking to people. He prided himself on coming to someone's rescue, sharing jokes (many of them I consider lame jokes but that's beside the point), and shooting the breeze with people. In keeping with these tendencies, as he started forming new memories and had mild level recall with his short term memory, we found him anxiously wanting to go visit his boss at work or find a reason for us to go anywhere out of the house. There was always someone he wanted to visit. The challenge was he wanted to act beyond his limitations and didn't realize he had limitations. He would say things inappropriate to the situation and sometimes would not be able to speak at all. Literally, his brain had the thoughts but he couldn't verbalize them. This, more than anything else, made him so incredibly frustrated. To protect him and prevent situations where he would say inappropriate things or get too overwhelmed and exhausted too quickly and go downhill, I tried limiting his outings when he was well enough to walk.

I remember my dad saying to my mom and me on multiple occasions that if he can't talk or verbalize his thoughts or worse—not make sense of his thoughts—he would rather be dead. I felt so helpless and couldn't imagine nor wanted to imagine what it would be like to be trapped in my own body and in my own head. A part of me might have felt the same way if I were in his shoes. To make matters worse, he couldn't write because of his brain injury and because his writing arm was badly injured in the accident.

My dad often felt useless. Here he was the primary caregiver for my disabled mom and provider for the family for over forty years and, in the blink of an eye, he was no longer able to do the things he used to do and was now dependent on others for everything. While I'd never been through this before, I tried putting myself in his shoes and did things to help him overcome these feelings. As he got somewhat stronger, I asked my dad to do little things like take the laundry basket to the laundry room, give the animal's food or water, carry papers to my mom, get me a glass of water; simple things like that. What I found was my dad started doing laundry. Now, you need to understand that my dad hadn't done his own laundry in decades. I didn't even ask and he was doing laundry. Then, as he gained more strength, he started doing dishes. Never mind that he would forget what was clean and what was dirty, he was doing dishes!

It was a constant struggle watching him try to do things beyond his capabilities, particularly when I spent time undoing things he was doing. For example, when he learned how to use the computer again and get around the Internet (dangerous), he would complete interest forms for countless schools and their programs. People would start calling and trying to recruit him to return to school. We started getting mail, catalogs, and things we didn't need. It was just more clutter! I had to ask some schools countless times to put his name and our number on their do not call list. He would just try doing it all over again, forgetting what he did previously. I kept his credit cards/bank cards away because he was impulsive and had no concept of what he was doing. This was a difficult blow to his ego but necessary for our family's protection.

Another example of his losing his independence and control over his life happened in March 2011, when I was out of town for work. He decided to get in their car and drive. He hadn't driven in over a year, not to mention seizures were now a way of life; in fact, he just had a seizure a week prior. My mom fell over her oxygen cords broke her ankle and was being taken to the hospital by ambulance. Thankfully, he didn't get into any accidents and everything and everyone was okay but his blood sugar plummeted while driving and he pulled off the side of the road before realizing he needed to eat. Struggling to drive and confused about where he was, he somehow went to Denny's to get something to eat. The fact he lied to Amanda about what he was doing told us he knew better than to get in the car and drive, but he did it anyway. He maintained, "Legally, I can drive." This was the first time he was alone and most certainly the first time he got behind the wheel of a car since his accident. Amanda was en route to get Felicity from work, get him, and visit my mom. One would think that if he went straight to the hospital, it halfway made sense; even knowing the risks. However, he didn't end up at the hospital.

I was at the Pittsburgh airport awaiting a flight home when Amanda and Felicity called to tell me what happened. I was so angry. I felt that if I talked to him, I was going to just go off on him. I knew he was brain injured and his frontal lobe was affected, but my goodness, to risk his life and the lives of others really affected me. As a result of this situation, I immediately contacted MVD[9], completed the form to revoke his driver's license, and that was the end of that. Now, he couldn't "legally drive." Given his respect for authority and the law, we hoped this kind of thing wouldn't happen again. The following day, I spent an hour yelling at him at the top of my lungs. I've NEVER yelled at my dad, ever—until this day. I found all my emotions spewing out of me and they just flowed like Niagara Falls. I was crying hysterically and couldn't stop my rants. Felicity tried to get me up to go outside and cool off and I wouldn't have it. Sarah ran into the family room, sat next to me and rubbed my back; reminding me to breathe the whole time. I was shaking, crying, yelling, and all the while was completely out of control. I wouldn't believe he would do something so incredibly stupid. I was so incredibly enraged that he would do something that could cause more injury to himself or worse, hurt or kill others. I kept reminding him of everything our family has been through since his accident. Bam, just like that, lives changed. When something happens to an individual, it's a whole ripple effect of impacted people. Lives changed in a flash. I asked him over and over why he would risk putting another family through what we've been through—or worse. I reminded him about the people who died in the same accident in 2009. Suddenly, I found myself feeling like I was throwing up words filled with rage. I wasn't just angry, I was seething with fury. I didn't realize just how much this impacted me. After I lost my voice ranting and raving and stopped shaking, I left the room for a bit. Sometime later, my dad carefully approached me, asked if it was okay to approach and gave me a hug. He apologized for his behavior.

---

[9] Motor Vehicle Division

My dad rarely apologized. I truly appreciated his gesture; particularly since he wasn't accustomed to showing his tender side much.

My dad felt like he was a burden. He didn't get emotional about much, but this he got emotional about. He would get visibly upset when talking about how no parent wants to be a burden on his or her children and he was sorry for being such a burden. I felt so sad for us all. He's family. He's my dad. Together with my mom, he brought me into this world. How could I think of him as a burden? Did I like the situation? No. Would I have chosen this situation on my own? Of course not. Did I want my house and all our lives turned upside down? Did I want them to lose their home, their freedom, their privacy and way of life? No. Did I want our lives turned upside down? Absolutely not. We did what we felt was right at the time.

Every single day was unpredictable. Actually, every hour of every day was unpredictable. We didn't know whether we would start or end a given day in an ER. We didn't know what day would be the last for my dad. Our schedule constantly changed. There were countless commitments missed. We lived day to day and sometimes, we lived hour to hour. With traumatic brain injuries, this is just the way of life. We didn't expect him to live a year. Once he hit around that mark was around the time his health started stabilizing and we felt we could breathe again.

While my dad suffered neurological brain damage, my mom also suffered. In addition to the myriad of physical conditions and managing the loss of the husband she knew, my mom suffered from paranoid schizophrenia. Schizophrenia is a mental disorder that makes it hard to tell the difference between what is real and not real; often thinking others are out to get them, including family members. It makes it difficult to have normal emotional responses to situations and people. During high periods of stress, affects of this disease reared its ugly head. Having lived with this since I was thirteen years old (when the disease first manifested), I was acutely aware of the signs and symptoms of her paranoia, depression, and hallucinations. I was so incredibly proud of my mom for handling everything going on with my dad and her own myriad of health challenges so well. She remained calm, balanced, and 'normal'. Then, around midyear 2010, I observed signs of her illness manifesting. It's almost as if now she felt that her husband was stable, she could 'relax' or maybe it was a delayed response. I'm not sure and it really doesn't matter why it happened. My mom started making comments about people, saying things or ask about that the rest of us couldn't hear. At first, it was subtle and I could tell as it got worse; she became bothered by it and tried hiding it. Then, my mom asked me to sit and talk with her. That's my sign she needed reassurance or advice about things. Out of the blue, she asked me why we were recording her moves in the house. Of course, we don't have video cameras or recording devices in the house monitoring her or anyone else's moves. "What has been said or done to make you think your moves are being watched?" I prodded. She replied, "It just seems that no matter what your dad and I do or no matter what we talk about, when it's just us and Amanda is in her room, she always knows. I think she watches us from her computer. After discussing examples of how my mom felt this way, I reassured her and gave her practical, logical, and real explanations, such as Amanda has good hearing and when she's in charge of watching over them, she is acutely aware of every noise for their protection. This is one of several such incidents we experienced. Sometimes, when my mom looked preoccupied or was particularly quiet, I gently asked if she was okay and watched for progressive mental health concerns.

Several times throughout her various hospital stays in 2010, she really felt unsafe and paranoid. Hospitals, especially if she was the patient, reminded her of stints at inpatient mental health facilities over the years. Between the time I was thirteen and twenty-one, my mom was in mental health hospitals three times, each time staying between one and three months. Hospitals reminded her of being like a prisoner, of being shackled to the bed, of losing control of her life. Her anxiety level got particularly high when social workers visited her. Social workers at the hospital talked of sending my mom to a home and this created even more anxiety. One time, when Amanda took my dad to the ER in Casa Grande (due to signs of brain bleeding), my mom refused to even step into the hospital. She stayed in the car for several hours by herself. Amanda checked on her periodically and gave her updates on my dad. She had a diaper on that day but for my mom to go two (2) hours without going to the bathroom, well, let's just say it's uncommon.. She's always had the bladder of an ant that has worsened with age. She had to go to the bathroom so bad and would move her body from side to side in her seat but there was no way in hell she was going inside that hospital to go to the bathroom.

I think what triggered her response in this situation was the fact that she was a patient in that hospital months prior for a week due to *another* broken ankle and her experience was still fresh in her mind. When my dad was in St. Joseph's hospital, my mom never hesitated visiting my dad. She either truly didn't mind or did a terrific job of overcoming her fears. Regardless, I am so proud of her for being so strong and showing unconditional love for my dad their entire marriage and in particular after his accident. I've never felt they were true soul mates, twin flames or whatever you want to call it, but they have always been a shining example of taking their vows seriously and literally. I believed it would be 'till death do you part' for them. I so admired how they cared for each other over the years. No matter what, they stuck by each other through thick and thin, for better or worse, richer or poorer, in sickness and in health.

My dad remained conflicted about his almost certain unpredictable future. One day, he acknowledged he/they would be with us until they either die or the level of care required exceeded our ability to care for them at home. Another day, he talked about getting a place of their own or moving in with Felicity. Then he talked about his Do Not Resuscitate (DNR) order and said no more surgeries, then he questioned why we would give up on him and back to him not wanting anymore surgeries and no more pain.

Sometimes, my dad relented and was resigned to the fact he wouldn't be able to work again, particularly in the field he had been in his entire career. His brain injuries negatively prevented him from performing the essential functions of his job as a Simulator Engineer. There were days he talked about returning to work or working at Wal-Mart as a greeter. Yeah, that would be fun to watch. He'd get in trouble for not letting shoppers shop because he'd stop everyone and talk with him or her for awhile.

When my dad talked about these things, I learned to either say nothing and listen or say something like, "That would be nice, Dad" or "I understand how or why you would want to do that." That seemed to help and then he forgot the conversation. I think he could let it go because he felt validated.

His inconsistent memory was challenging. Some days, he recalled things—some little and some big—and other days, he asked the same thing multiple times and wouldn't remember whatever it was. This proved challenging as a caregiver. I didn't want to talk down to him or treat him like he was "less than." Conversely, I didn't want to assume he "got it" only to discover he didn't get it.

There are many more examples of ways my parent's needed to have the space and time to learn daily acts of living and 'being' in general. I hope this gives you a sense of the types of challenges my parents faced every single day. Then there were seemingly little things like getting bathed, dressed, and eating, which we'll explore in the Family Action Guide section below.

KEY LESSONS LEARNED

1. *We didn't take everything my dad said literally.* We realized he still tried putting the puzzle pieces together and, in doing so, mixed up memories, fact, and fiction. When we agreed with his ideas or said "That would be nice, Dad," he seemed less agitated. I think this approach helped heal. By validating his feelings and affirming something positive, he felt heard and let go of the thought.

2. *The TV and Internet were not his friends;* although he thought they were his friends. TV and Internet added to his confusion and, as we later discovered, can be contributing factors for seizures. As explained to me, this was due to the flashing changes of scenes and lights from the TV or monitor. They were also bad for him because it created further confusion with more ideas and stories in his head. Too much TV and computer

time confused his brain and caused eye fatigue easier than other activities.

3. *We learned to pick our battles* and let him do things as long as there wasn't a threat of injury. We slowly integrated things for him to do around the house. This made him feel needed and, I am certain, aided in his overall healing and well-being.

4. *I trusted and acted on my intuition when communicating.* I let go of any particular outcome and remembered that everything happening was all in divine order.

5. *I put post-it reminders* around the house to remind my dad of things.

6. *On tough days, I took deep breaths, breathing in and out* several times and thought very carefully before I spoke. We didn't assume the last conversation about something was the end all and I involved them in their care and associated decisions. Never assume!

7. *We allowed them to just be.* If it took an hour for my dad to get a shirt on and he was OK working through it himself, it was fine with us. This, of course, provided, we weren't on a deadline to be somewhere.

FAMILY ACTION GUIDE

1. Allow your loved one as much independence as possible. It may be painful to watch. Allow it anyway. An example of this in action is bathing, shaving, dressing and overall body cleanliness. I've heard people share situations where their loved one decided to go on strike with showers, baths, and cleansing themselves. It sounds odd yet in reality, this was something they had control over and it bothered everyone around them more than it bothered the person on strike, and

that's the way the rebellious person likes it! Having frank conversations about the emotions involved in how they are caring for themselves, within their limitations of course, is important.

2. Be patient. Remember that disagreements are a part of life and failing memory tends to occur with age. Exercise extreme patience and compassion with each other.

3. Make your loved one(s) a part of the entire household. Include them in discussions and daily life.

4. Swiftly address and minimize potential safety and legal liability issues with mobility such as driving. This is an area that you, as their caregiver and advocate, must ensure their safety and the safety of those around them. It is a balancing act. Sometimes the wheelchair *is* the independence. This is bigger than their emotions, pride, freedom and wants. There are ethical and legal issues involved here. In such circumstances, we must take swift action to ensure everyone's safety.

5. Mobility issues such as when to use a walker, wheelchair, power chair or other medical equipment is important to discuss with your loved one. We struggled getting my dad to use a walker inside the house. He thought there were enough walls to keep him upright. This is a sensitive issue because this weighs on their independence and dependence. Particularly when they feel out of control and there are behavioral issues, this can be challenging at best. To address this, we did the following:

    a. We installed ramps in and outside the house for easy access via walker, wheelchair, etc…

    b. We encouraged the use of walkers with my dad. My mom vacillated between using a walker and wheelchair but she was able to assess her abilities and realized her limitations.

c. When my dad wasn't using a walker, we physically walked him where he needed to go. He didn't like that anymore than he liked having a walker. However, he was such a high fall risk, this was crucial for his safety. We also had a gait belt that went around his chest/abdominal area that we used to help him from point A to point B. Eventually, my dad recognized that his safety was more important than his need for independence and he started using his walker.

d. Remove all rugs and anything else that could cause someone to trip, slip or fall.

6. Treat and help patients (in my case someone with traumatic brain injury) with respect and be cognizant of everything you say and do to prevent them from feeling inferior. I could have used the strategies above from the start. We spent so much time trying to correct him, repeat things, and set the record straight, that it confused him more. Very early on during his first rehabilitation stay and when he made the largest chunks of recovery, I found writing on the board and repeating things over and over and over and over again helped him remember. At that stage, though, this strategy hurt more than helped him —mentally and emotionally. Much of what he communicated about the last year wasn't from his memory; it was from what we told him about what happened. There is a distinct difference and you wouldn't know it from talking with him.

7. Demonstrate effective communication strategies in general. These include:

a. Use "I" statements to share your feelings and to mirror back what the other person said. Some examples include saying things like: "I realize, however...," "I hear what you are saying," "I understand," "I feel xxx," "If I understood you right, what I heard you say is "....". Is that right?

b. Practice active listening skills. Communication is 2/3 listening!

c. When repeating back something, be sure to use the same language they used to communicate with you.

d. Refrain from interpreting what they are trying to say.

e. Come from a place of win-win. One person doesn't have to be wrong for the other person to be right.

f. Realize it's OK to 'agree to disagree' sometimes.

g. Share the feelings underneath your concerns. Refrain from becoming attached to any particular position on the subject.

8. Demonstrating consistency and tough love with a compassionate heart is of utmost importance for healing. At first, I had a structured schedule with exercises and such for him to do daily. I did my best to mimic the structured hospital environment. However, as time went on and it seemed that his brain was likely the best it was going to get, I eased off a bit. Watching TV, being on the computer and reading were ingrained in him as long as I've known him. Given everything else he lost control over, I felt eliminating his favorite things in life would have hurt everyone.

9. Lead the way and support dietary needs. Issues of what to eat, when to eat, portion size and ability to feed oneself are important issues that will likely require discussion. My parent's were diabetic and required specific dietary restrictions. Amanda cooked 90% of the time. Another issue with food is ensuring everything a loved one needs is reachable. This may require shifting cabinet space to accommodate everyone's capabilities.

10. Be sensitive to physical, emotional, mental and spiritual support needs. I could have been more sensitive to my mom's support needs when she stayed at the hospital. For the most part, every time she was in the hospital, so was my dad. I felt like I treated my parent's unequally and often felt my mom thought I cared more for my dad. This certainly wasn't the case. Their health situations were just very different and required different care strategies. I was making life and death decisions about my dad's care. He didn't recognize people outside of our immediate family and he listened to me. He couldn't play a proactive role in his health and I was his advocate. I needed to be there more to ensure I talked with doctors about his care. He was touch and go. My mom wasn't. My mom was capable of communicating her health symptoms with medical professionals and I was able to rely more on my sister to visit her. The various times my mom was in the hospital in 2010, half of her stays were at the Casa Grande hospital while the other half of her hospital stays were at a local hospital. Proximity certainly made a difference as well (1 ½ hours vs. 20 minutes round trip) and the Casa Grande hospital was on Felicity's way home from work.

11. Allow patients to have mistakes or delays along the way and allow independence; where appropriate. We felt that most things my parents did or tried to do around the house or with self-care took a lot longer without assistance. Nevertheless, when they felt they were able to clean up one of their messes or perform simple daily acts of living, we let them do it. Sometimes, it took them hours to do something we could have helped them do within about 15 minutes…and that was okay. This was part of the journey and road to healing. Allowing them to do things themselves that don't pose a risk demonstrates respect and preserves their dignity.

12. Similar to numbers 1 and 9 above, an important issue is dressing yourself. Once my dad was able to perform acts of

daily living, it often took him 30 minutes to an hour to get his shirt on. Sometimes he put shirts on inside out. Who cares? If this happens, let the person be. The more you try to control the situation, the more they will resist your efforts, resent you or plain flat do things just to get back at you.

13. A prevalent issue for my mom was toilet care. She had a bedside portable potty chair she used 100% of the time. Sometimes, she was in so much pain, it would take her ½ hour to get up out of bed and get to her toilet. We offered help yet often she would say she is getting there and manage herself. She would sometimes sit on the toilet for hours at a time because she wasn't entirely ready to tackle getting back to bed. My mom did ask for help when she felt she really needed it. Otherwise, we let her be.

14. Meet them where they are. This can be interpreted on all levels and all situations.

CHAPTER NINE

Keeping Your Loved Ones Safe and Activities Families Can Share

"I did then what I knew how to do. Now that I know better, I do better."

~ Maya Angelou

We don't know what we don't know until we know we don't know it.

I just thought the accident changed everything. THIS changed everything. This subject needs to be front and center on a national level platform. Keeping loved ones safe is about ensuring they are safe physically, emotionally, and financially. For purposes of this book, I am including neglect and abandonment in emotional and physical well-being. I acknowledge there are a lot of amazing, caring, selfless people and organizations providing outstanding quality senior care. Each family needs to select what works best for them and their needs.

Usually, the first time a person considers this is when an event triggers the need to evaluate options for short and/or long term care of a loved one. This was certainly one of my key initial concerns after my dad's accident. We had to decide fairly quickly after my dad's accident whether to keep my parents in their home, move them to my home, hire someone privately in their home, or put them in an appropriate facility. There are lots of options for providing short and long term care of a loved one. They can be in an assisted living facility, a nursing home, provide full time or intermittent home health care/nursing care or care for them yourself/as a family. One of THE most important care giving factors for families is how to keep loves ones safe at all times.

Every situation is different. On average, annual costs for these options for *us* ranged from $60,000 to $120,000. This was after taxes and only included facility costs, meals and most activities, but not additional medical costs. Oh my Gosh. Who the hell is going to pay for this? Isn't there a special 'home in the sky' that takes care of people? Will "they" take care of everything so I can work? Will "they" manage their care? What about Medicare? This includes direct costs, prescriptions, supplies, doctor co-pays, lab fees, surgeries, equipment, deductibles; the list alone could be another book and doesn't include the hefty emotional price for those in need and their caregivers.

Elder abuse is a significant problem.[10] In the United States alone, over 500,000 older adults are believed to be abused or neglected each year. These statistics are likely a low estimate because many victims are unable or afraid to tell anyone about the abuse. I have heard that most seniors fear nursing homes more than they do death itself. According to My elder advocate, indeed there is no greater fear for an elderly person than being placed in a nursing home – even on a short-term basis. This fear is well founded. The Federal Government admits that 45% of our 16,000 nursing homes are substandard. Another 25% of our nursing homes are labeled as "average."

The consequences of being in a bad nursing home can lead to ongoing pain, depression, and death. I visited some of these places. I understand the fear. I wouldn't want to be in one of these 70% of homes the Federal Government says are either substandard or average. With very little notice and a lot of knowledge to catch up on, I worked with Professor Google in search of how these facilities were evaluated, how they fared, what questions to ask and got my list together. I visited some of these places unexpectedly. I purposely showed up unannounced like a mom evaluating day care centers. It's what you see when people aren't prepared for your arrival that I wanted to see. I understood the pain. I could feel some residents yearning for attention, care, love, and companionship. I saw patients needing a blanket or a drink and the list goes on. I smelled death. I felt fear and loneliness.

After visiting the second facility, I cried in my car. I couldn't believe people lived like that; as if they are just waiting to die. In some cases, I saw people just starring off yonder in their wheelchair. And sterile rooms with metal furniture with very little space for personal items and even less privacy was the norm. Most rooms were shared

---

[10] Department of Health and Human Services – National Center on Elder Abuse

and they weren't quite as small as an inside room cruise ship where you have to walk sideways to get by anything but it was sure darn close. Now, don't get me wrong, there were some absolutely fabulous places; places I wanted to live. The catch? These places cost money and lots of it. It was money we didn't have to spend.

After putting people through the ringer with questions, I felt so sad for the average person who needs quality nursing home care and doesn't have the money, insurance coverage or an advocate looking out for their well-being. I felt bad for families trying to get quality care for their parents from afar. I felt bad for the high quality senior care facilities who work hard to ensure patients' safety and for being associated with a group of facilities that give nursing homes and assisted living homes a bad name. Aside from logistics and cost, there was the issue that my mom's medical care needs were of a physical and mental nature and my dad's needs were of a neurological and physical nature. When I looked into things, they would have been separated based on their individual care needs.

This part of the chapter addresses key things to look for when evaluating nursing homes.

Evaluating Short and Long-Term Care Facilities

Things to look for:

1. Poor nutrition. Additionally, check for food quality. If the food doesn't taste good, our loved ones probably won't eat it.

2. Overmedication. Watch for accurate medication and dosages as well as any signs of anti-psychotic drug use that can sometimes be used for hard to manage patients.

3. Infections. Watch for a clean environment all around. Also, watch for bedsores. Patients lying in the same position in bed for hours or days at a time are at high risk for developing bedsores. If not treated, bedsores can cause serious health issues up to and including death.

4. Poor staffing. This includes looking at both the quality and quantity of staff.

5. Isolation. This is one of the most prevalent ways patients become at risk for physical abuse and depression.

6. Physical abuse. This includes any signs of things like bruises or broken bones.

7. Financial abuse. Nursing/Assisted living care patients are often at risk for financial scams. Watch and protect.

8. Financial abuse. Watch all bills for accurate medical, prescriptions and health care provider charges.

9. Discuss roles, responsibilities and expectations with hospital administration before your loved one is admitted. Issues such as medical management, continuity of care, transportation, to doctor updates, or emergency room policies and procedures, eviction policies, off site family time restrictions, laundry process, on site amenities and costs, outside food policies and insurance communication are all vitally important to know before your loved one is admitted.

10. Check out facility ratings online. Check for any complaints and ratings. What is the nature of the complaints? Find out about employee turnover. These are a few places to start.

11. Is the facility Medicare and Medicaid certified?

12. What is the occupancy rate?

13. Are they accepting new patients and is there a waiting period?

14. Is the facility AND administrator licensed?

15. In addition to initial background checks for staff, does the facility conduct ongoing background checks? If so, what information is checked and what are facility hiring standards?

16. What training is in place for all staff?

17. Is there a disaster and evacuation plan? How often is it reviewed with staff?

18. Does the facility have various activities that patients can choose from such as cards, bingo, reading, art, music and the like?

19. Does the facility have outdoor areas for patient use? If so, what is the protocol for patient safety outdoors? Is there an outdoor staff to patient ratio?

20. Is the facility free from smells, obstructions, dirt and disorganization?

21. Are care plan meetings held at times that are easy for residents and their family members to attend?

22. Does the facility have outside volunteers that come in for activities or pet therapy? If so, what background requirements are they held to?

23. After checking recent state reports, inquire about remediation for any and all deficiencies on the report.

24. Are patients offered a variety of meal options? If so, how is food consumed verified against any dietary requirements/restrictions?

25. Are there optional services available such as on site haircuts? If so, what are the costs and how does administration work with family to ensure services rendered are within budget?

26. Who is involved in decisions regarding restraints?

27. Do patients have enough time to eat? Can they select their own dining schedule?

28. Are there adequate safety features around the facility such as hand rails, grab bars, lowered mirrors, smoke detectors, sprinklers, security, bed alarms, etc...?

Remember, nursing home admissions staff look at one aspect of patient eligibility. Full communication with appropriate parties is essential to ensuring your loved one gets the best care. This includes having a thorough assessment of your loved one's physical and cognitive health to ensure a good match with their needs and a facility's abilities. All of these nursing home safety tips and home safety times can be applied to each other.

Regardless of where a loved one is being cared for, there are common safety considerations every person needs to address. People's homes weren't designed to be in a hospital friendly floor plan. As you already know, we decided that as long as their needs didn't exceed our capabilities, we would keep them at our home. This impacted my career, my children's college, retirement and so much more. I didn't have time to prepare for any of this, yet I had to make time.

Some call it 'baby proofing' and the kids called it 'grandpa proofing'. We installed locks and alarms on all exits to alert us when anything opened. Suddenly, I found myself putting notes around the house for my dad, reminding him of what to NOT put in the microwave. What do you do when your father walks outside with keys, underwear, and socks thinking he can drive somewhere? What do you do when your dad won't listen to your mother about critical safety issues? How do you keep your dad from tripping over your mother's oxygen cord strewn about the house? How do you prevent your father from talking to someone on the phone trying to take advantage of him financially when he clearly can't speak coherently; particularly when he is trying to act beyond his capabilities? How do you help your mother keep her feet elevated or get to the bathroom in time when she wants to be at the computer all day?

The rest of this chapter addresses the tsunami of issues and considerations for overall safety of a loved one at home. Specifically, I will address physical, emotional and financial safety with some stories along the way. It is organized into two sections:

Ensuring home physical, emotional and financial safety with some stories along the way.

Safety considerations for nursing home patients.

Keeping Loved Ones Safe at Home

Physical Safety:

1. Door handles. We installed door handles because we couldn't have any more falls or injury. We installed bathroom handrails and installed raised (handicap grade) toilet seats for greater accessibility.

2. Wheel chair ramps. We installed wheelchair ramps in various places around the house for easier maneuvering.

3. We got extended grabbers. Think of those long grab handles that allow someone to open and grab for reaching difficult items.

4. We moved utensils and food within reach.

5. For my dad, we put vital information together, including his name, addresses, medical conditions, medications, allergies, and emergency instructions. We put this in a pouch around his neck when outside the house. A wallet size paper with key information also works. I adapted this from a tip I got from a friend and colleague. Thank you, Anna.

6. Bedside ringers. We got loud bells for their bedside so they could ring for us.

7. Alarm system. We added a medical emergency button to our home alarm system and had a portable device they could use to alert medical personnel. We ensured our alarm system beeped loudly when any doors or windows opened. The system announced what was opening so we knew what part of the house to go. For example, my dad convinced my mom early on to sneak out of the house to go eat. This is dangerous for them. It's dangerous for us. It's dangerous for others on the road. If they get on the road and hurt someone there could have been legal implications. He could barely walk and she was in no shape to drive. Steven followed them out the front door and told them to come back inside. They didn't listen. Steven ran in to get Amanda and she ran outside and brought them back in the house. She later took them where they wanted to go.

8. Phones. Here are some suggestions. Buy a pay as you go phone so if it gets lost or dropped in water, it's okay. We added a basic line to our family plan for $10 a month so my mom had a basic phone to use.

9. Wash hands often. We could have bought stock in instant hand sanitizer. There were bottles everywhere. Before and after doing anything, we washed our hands and, at times, arms, neck, or other appropriate parts of the body exposed to germs, infections, etc… We used both instant sanitizer and regular hand soap to ensure as germ free a home as possible and minimize skin dryness.

10. Wash reusable supplies. We followed the same practice as number nine above.

11. Meals. Make sandwiches or other easily made and kept meals. We made and served meals for them so they didn't need to use any kitchen appliances. My mom couldn't cook before but she would use a microwave. We avoided having my dad use a

microwave until further along in recovery. One day, we found my dad trying to put things in the oven that could have caught fire had we not caught it in time.

12. Walkers, wheelchairs, canes, and oxygen. We encouraged the use of a cane and walker for my dad when he was at various recovery stages. My mom, having broken her foot several times between 2010 and 2012, needed to use her walker for rehabilitation. Some days, she would only walk two steps…they were two steps in the right direction! When you can get multiples of walkers or wheelchairs and your vehicle allows for it, I strongly recommend it. While you are at it, put labels with your name on everything. When you are at the hospital, your walker, wheelchair, oxygen concentrator and the like can get lost among the hospital walkers and such. Yes, it happens! It happened to us several times. Fortunately, they were found because we had our name on our equipment.

13. Move slowly. We encouraged my parents to slowly sit, lie down or rise as the case may be.

14. Beds. We ensured their bed was as low as they needed it to be and that the wheels were safely locked in place.

15. Furniture. We moved furniture around to minimize my mom's oxygen cord from getting stuck.

16. Foot elevation. We got good elevation rests for my parents to use while they were in a sitting position yet needed their feet up. Extra chairs or wheelchairs worked well for this, too. When my mom was recovering from foot or ankle breaks and diabetic ulcer infections, her wheel chair legs were incredibly helpful. It helped keep her legs elevated and protected them from getting banged up by people or things.

17. Medications. My mom and I put my dad's medications together in daily pill containers with labeled days of the week. We monitored

medication intake. At times, medications were in the form of liquid, creams, or gels. This required additional calendar tracking. Then, we put all medication bottles away so he didn't double dose or confuse things. This single thing made our lives easier.

18. Blood sugar tracking. We wrote down blood sugar and blood pressure levels and took this information with us to doctors' appointments.

19. Accessible microwave. We bought a user friendly microwave and placed on the counter for easy wheelchair access.

20. Food accessibility and preparation. We bought an egg boiler, a little omelet maker, and things like microwavable steamed vegetables so my mom had some level of independence in preparing simple foods.

21. Backscratcher. If you've ever had a back itch, you know how valuable a backscratcher is!

22. Cups. We bought non-glass cups with large handles for easy grabbing.

23. Refrigerator. We ensured foods they needed were placed on accessible shelves.

24. Power company notification. We notified our electric company that we had an oxygen dependent person in the home. This proved to be valuable for several reasons. First, the company tagged our home as a priority in the event of electric service downtime. Second, they provided a disability discount.

25. Night lights. We used night-lights around the home for adequate lighting.

26. Stable furniture. We made sure breakable items were removed from high standing furniture such as entertainment centers,

bookcases, and dressers. In some cases, we removed furniture posing an accident risk.

27. Front door. Consider wheelchair bound people and placing a peephole within eye reach so they can see who is at the front door.

28. Neighbors. For those living at home requiring periodic care, sometimes having a trusted neighbor who can either check on them or establish a process to let the neighbor know you are up and okay. One way to do this is to flip blinds open or some other sign visible from the neighbor's home.

29. Cars. Whether you are car shopping or looking to update an existing car to meet your driving or passenger needs, take the following into consideration:

    a.   Angle of the front doors. Some are narrower at the bottom for foot entry.

    b.   Leg room to accommodate supplies for easy access.

    c.   Door handles to grab onto when maneuvering in and out of the car.

    d.   Easy to use seatbelts. We all know how challenging seatbelts can get and how much force it can take to actually get buckled!

    e.   Height of the car. Some need lower cars to get into while others need higher cars for easy access. If possible, have the person test these things when considering a car purchase.

    f.   Customized driving settings.

    g.   Back up camera and distance alerts. I have seen far too many elderly drivers back up without looking behind them. For that matter, I've seen far too many people in general backing up without checking their environment. One thing I have witnessed time and time again with elderly in my own family and strangers alike is accidently hitting parked cars in front of them when parking. When someone's ability to calculate distance, depth and perception when behind the wheel is negatively affected - accidents happen. Discussions about the appropriateness of driving is probably in order.

h. Disability parking license plate or rear few mirror insignia. If you have one consistently driven car, I recommend getting a license plate versus a removable placard. It is one less thing to remember and maximizes driving visibility should one forget to remove the placard to drive.

i. Easy to open and close doors and trunk.

j. Power chair and wheel chair storage and ramp accessibility.

All of this sounds easy enough, right? It all costs money and required a great deal of time.

Emotional Safety:

1. Communication. We coached my mom to develop her voice and learn how to say no to my dad. This proved difficult the more belligerent he became. It was also challenging because of the lifetime communication patterns between them. We worked hard to increase communication with my mom and give her status updates on our household comings and goings; being particularly cognizant of her mental conditions and periodic symptoms. She needed to feel safe and secure. We also had periodic family meetings to address any issues, communicate updates, share what's working and what's not and ensure everyone was on the same page.

2. Mail management. The sad reality of the situation when a parent's health declines is they are no longer able to make appropriate decisions about what to buy or where to put the mail. Important mail could make its way to a bookshelf between, above or below books never to be found. Cancel unneeded mail, ensure mail is forwarded, follow up on all requests and keep documentation of said requests. I fielded all the mail. Prior to my mom's illness and my dad's accident, they subscribed to countless magazines and would receive mounds of catalogs. My parents were compulsive shoppers, but, I believe in part it was because it provided them a sense of purpose. An example of this compulsive behavior was when my dad purchased over $7,000 worth of learning CD's over a two-year period from a catalog. In the process of cleaning out their homes, we found three big boxes worth of these materials form the same company. In some cases, he purchased three and four sets of the same thing and 98 percent of these were unwrapped. Mind you, the CD's weren't found together. They were collectively in different places across two homes, a storage unit, and their garage. Amanda cataloged everything and sent it all back with a nice cover letter my mom drafted. The company CEO sent a check to us with a letter indicating that while they honor their 100 percent refund policy with no time limits, we were not allowed to ever order from them again. We were fine with this. To this day, we still receive their catalogs. I tossed them before my dad saw them! One time, a catalog slipped by me and he was literally clutching this catalog to his chest. I saw it and immediately jumped out of my chair, grabbed it, and tossed it in the trash. He sulked for a few hours, and I realized perhaps I overreacted a bit, but all I could think about when I saw the catalog in his hands were the countless hours and wasted money dealing with those darn CD's.

3. Advocate. We served as their voice,their advocate and stood up for what they needed. I handled the vast, massive, frustrating and ongoing myriad of calls on their behalf for everything.

4. Outings. We took them places out of the house; especially for special occasions like their wedding anniversary. We made special reservations for their 44th anniversary dinner in June 2011. They absolutely loved this!

5. Self-care. I made sure my mom periodically had her hair done and nails manicured. This helped her feel special. We got my dad his first and last pedicure. I had a friend who does massage come to the house and give my dad a massage. He really, really appreciated that.

6. Legacy. This is so important that there is an entire chapter in this book dedicated to legacy. My mom loved telling stories and would talk to anyone who would listen. My dad stayed in his head. He was always more of a 'mental' person in that his mind was constantly churning and it was difficult to move him from his head to his heart. To say drawing out and documenting life stories and things that were important to them helped their emotional well-being is an understatement. This was probably one of the key things that allowed our entire family to have peace with everything. We had the incredible gift of time with them to share these stories and carry them forward to future generations.

7. Boundaries and conditions. It is important to establish what your conditions are as a caregiver and what you will and won't accept; ahead of time, if at all possible. Recognizing what you have control over versus having influence over is important. Further, ensuring you agree on all conditions is imperative for everyone's well-being and prevents arguments down the road.

8. Expressions of support and love. We supported each other in countless ways through our hugs, talks, listening and being a sounding board, general support, compassion and gratitude. My parents weren't very affectionate nor did they make it a practice to say "I love you" as I grew up. I knew they loved me. They just didn't say it much. Can you relate to a situation in childhood

that was a defining moment or building of moments where you said to yourself when you had a family, you were going to always X or never Y? I'm sure we've all had these defining moments. Somewhere along the way, verbal expressions of love became something I was going to do differently when I had kids. Having us all in this cozy home and integrating our two very different ways of operating and being proved challenging at times. It required love, patience, acceptance and faith.

9. Merging lives and households. Imagine merging two already full households; households each with their own daily practices, their own traditions, acceptable noise levels, communication styles, religious practices, pets, sleeping habits, and competing resources such as computer use and bathroom use! There is a lot of dynamics at play here. We all exercised compassion and love with each other every step of the way. One area that took me almost a year to come to grips with was whether my mom's three cats could migrate to our home. When my mom moved in with us (my dad was in the hospital during this time but technically he moved in too; he just didn't know it yet) their three cats went with Felicity. Felicity already had 2 cats. I figured I had our parents and she got their pets. Fair trade, right? Things were so unsettled for so long and integrating our human, feline and canine family was already overwhelming for me. I couldn't fathom having yet another animal; much less three additional animals. It simply didn't equate. As time went on, I realized just how much my mom really needed the companionship and unconditional love her felines provided. After almost a year, I finally agreed she could bring ONE cat to our house. That's where I drew the line. Her special Siamese cat, Carmine, joined our family. Instantly, I felt my mom's emotional and mental tank rising before my eyes. With everything she had been through, she, too, needed a constant in her life. She needed a companion. Someone who wouldn't yell or argue and someone that she could entertain for hours at a time. To this day, Carmine remains in our home. I

see what she saw in him and I'm so thankful to have Carmine in our lives. He is one special cat.

Financial Safety:

1. Financial planning. We had advance directives, power of attorney and wills documented and shared with the appropriate parties.

2. Free or reduced medication costs. Many pharmaceutical companies offer deep discounts or free medications through prescription assistance programs. Go to the manufacturer websites for any medications needed and see if they have such programs. These companies give millions of dollars worth of medications free each year. Another site to check is www.needymed.com. This is a consolidated site for consumers needing deeply discounted medications.

3. Negotiated medical bills. Some medical provider expenses can be negotiated at a much lower cost. If you don't have insurance, or you have a deductible that's beyond your means, check with your providers to see if they will work with you. More often than not, they have patient assistance programs and are happy to help. They want to get paid and you want to fulfill your obligation. It's a win-win.

4. Joint accounts. Be VERY careful about having any joint accounts with the loved one being cared for if you otherwise wouldn't have had joint accounts. There are implications for financial responsibility resting on your shoulders. In short, you are likely liable for the debt. In my experience and with one exception, having a POA on record doesn't mean you must be added to your loved one's financial accounts. This issue certainly warrants discussion.

5. Multiple insurance providers. Having multiple insurance providers doesn't always mean better coverage. We found insurance companies continually making the other companies primary; which created a lot of delays getting bills paid. If you have multiple insurance carriers, I strongly recommend working with coordination of benefits for each provider and ensuring everyone is on the same page with which insurance company is primary, secondary, etc...

6. Coupons. It may sound obvious but coupons are a good money saver. For example, my parents needed to drink Ensure. This is extremely expensive and sniffing out coupons for this product saved considerably over time. I found the resources at www.daveramsey.com to be tremendously helpful. He has quite a few tips to help everyone. Lozo.com, coupondivas.com, couponcode.com and groupon.com are some of my favorite coupon sites. Of course, another resource is Professor Google. You'd be surprised at the coupons out there just waiting for you.

7. Student loan forgiveness. If your loved one has outstanding student loans, requesting a forbearance helps extend the time to repay loans and can provide temporary relief. In the event of permanent disability, you can request a disability discharge. In our case, because the my dad was so touch and go and we weren't sure of the final outcome, his student loan companies conditionally discharged the debt until such time passed that my dad was rendered permanently disabled and ultimately discharged the debt completely. After death, you can request debts be discharged for credit card outstanding balances. It's not easy but it is worth the time.

8. When evaluating nursing home options and if you opt to have a nursing home manage funds, find out if trust funds managed on their behalves are insured. An unfortunate growing trend is nursing home patient fund thefts. Be diligent in reviewing all

monies for appropriate allocation. Find out what checks and balances the facility has to ensure financial compliance.

9. Seek legal counsel to evaluate your financial situation and needs. I recommend an attorney specializing in elder care/family care *and* estate planning.

10. Evaluate and decide on after death arrangements. Having these details handled before death ensures your needs are met and makes it easier for those afterwards.

11. Daily money management. Have a budget and be on the same page with your spouse/partner. I managed my parents' finances initially and turned some of the reins over to my mom for a period of time. It took me months in early 2010 to get recurring charges, some of which were fraudulent, stopped by the various merchants. It was a painful process and one I wish on nobody. In early 2011, when my dad 'just wanted to go deposit a check—in person,' Amanda took my dad to the bank. He was stable with his walker during this time, and Amanda respected his wishes to go in the bank alone. At his request, he got another bank cad. He thought he could sneak it by me. The next month on their bank statement, I started seeing recurring expenses for $29.99 and $19.99 monthly for credit score monitoring and ID protection. *Wow*, I thought, *here we go again*. And again, I spent time reversing these charges. You may be wondering why we weren't on the same page with what we allowed and didn't. You see, there is a distinct difference between an adult daughter who is a caregiver and a young adult granddaughter who is a caregiver. At times, Amanda felt it was important to let her grandpa have some sense of independence. She respected her elders and she felt bad for him. Sometimes, she felt stuck between a rock and a hard place.

Many of my parent's financial issues happened before my dad's accident. Because of his injuries, confronting him would have been detrimental, as he didn't remember or confused things. The more I uncovered with my dad's accounts, the more I realized my dad didn't practice what he preached. This was a huge shift for me and, for the first time in my life, I found myself feeling disappointed in my dad and sad that he would do such things. One particular day late December 2009, I spent an hour at a local bank where my dad had overdrawn his individual account by more than $1,600 in less than a month. My goal was to eliminate future fees and close all accounts. I paid the $1,600 with my own money but did anyone realize how this impacts my household? I didn't have an extra $1,600 lying around. You see, my dad worked hard over the years to 'hide' money from my mom and told people that if there were money in the joint account, she would spend every last penny. What we didn't know about my dad was it was his spending habits that were out of control. My mom was a spender, too, but she spent a fraction of his spending. And here we thought all these years she was spending their financial future away. He obviously didn't count on being in a car accident. The frustrating thing about this situation is he had no recall of how he spent all this money and, when we told and showed him things we discovered; he had an explanation that made perfect sense to him.

"Consider how hard it is to change yourself and you'll understand what little chance you have in trying to change others."

~ Jacob M. Braude

12. Watch out for sneaky online spending. Watch for expenses from online merchants such as bill you later or PayPal. It didn't do much good to take my mom's cards away when she had her information stored with online merchants. In particular, she used services allowing her to be billed later for things. That way, I didn't see the bank transactions. I didn't want to treat my mom like a child, yet, at times, she acted like one. I remember reminding her to stop spending—no more cat stuff—no more gadgets; there was no room for these things anyway. For the first time in my life, I saw my mom sulk. Her lower lip protruded out and she frowned, saying "I need my

money…my mad money…my fun money." I said, "Really, Mom. You guys aren't receiving income and you want mad money. Look around—there is no mad money. There is no space for more 'stuff' in the house. Stop it!" For a while, I took her bank access away but soon realized she had a special way of getting bills paid and it did give her something to do, a contribution and burden lifted from me. We monitored things to ensure unexpected charges didn't creep up.

Just as kids can do this and want to feel freedom so can parents who want their freedom when they feel they've lost it.

> *"Whether you think you can or think you can't, you're right."*
> *~ Henry Ford*

Activities Families Can Share

Once the critical issue of safety is addressed, one of the next things caregivers want to know are activities families can share.

Nothing can make you feel helpless like watching your father, your hero and someone you've always learned from, stare at a telephone like it's a foreign object or watch him learn how to count money again. From playing the memory game to simple math problems, to puzzles to spending the afternoon talking about the good old days, in this section, I share specific games and activities that helped improve my dad's memory recall. Emphasis on the stages of healing and how families can make learning fun, bond, and help their loved one is addressed. lessons learned, like the power silence has to give someone the extra time they need to think and a family action guide, including specific strategies I used to improve my dad's cognitive function and recommended general activities to do together.

Activities and therapeutic games we worked on with my dad to improve memory recall and social interaction included:

Mental and Cognitive Well-Being:

1. Simple, elementary school-level math problems. Counting coins and graduating to simple math word problems to reinforce money learning.

2. Problem Solving and Strategy games. Chess, Mastermind, Risk, and Rummikub all hone problem solving skills.

3. Matching and word recall games. Scattergories, Boggle, Ad Libs, Taboo, and Scrabble are all effective games for word recall. We would show him sets of cards on the table, let him study it for a few minutes, turn the cards over, and see how many cards he could match. Another fun game included giving him six to eight words to memorize and let him study them and say them. Then, we covered the page and asked him to circle the previous words again, adding sixteen or so other words. Then we switched the order of the sixteen words and asked him to circle the words previously seen again.

4. Attention games. Solitaire, Sudoku, and crossword puzzles were all stellar activities my dad loved to evolve his attention capacity. These activities also help mental flexibility.

5. Reading a page or chapter and having him recall and summarize key events from the chapter. As noted earlier, my dad discovered he liked rereading books to see how much he remembered. This works when you remember what you remember. Nonetheless, it is a helpful strategy.

6. Visual and spatial games. Rush Hour, Sudoku, Crosswords, Mankala, and Kings in Corners are other games to help with this.

7. Speech therapy.

8. A tremendous wealth of information and brain games is available on www.luminocity.com. I strongly recommend this

site for everyone. After all, if you are like me, sometimes we need memory boosters after going to one room for something, forgetting what you went there for, returning to the previous room, sitting down and then it hits you. For some of us, the process repeats itself over and over. I've known people ages 17 – 70 who benefited from their offerings.

Physical Well-Being:

1. My dad practiced moving his right arm to his side and over his head. He never made it that far and we were concerned about muscle atrophy. Being in hospital beds off and on for close to six (6) months, despite periodic physical therapy, it was close to impossible for him to regain full use of his arm. Still, we encouraged him to work through the pain and use one-pound weights and home exercise equipment to improve arm function.

2. He used stretch bands, like the kind used for Pilates or yoga, to stretch his arms and chest. These exercises helped him initially more than anything else to get to his eventual arm function plateau. Of course, all physical activities such as these were approved by his physical therapist. We merely encouraged him to do these activities to increase recovery and mobility.

Emotional Well-Being:

1. With all these activities noted above, we were more patient, allowing him extra time to sit in silence as he figured things out. This extra space gave him the safe space and support to release frustrations and allow the exercises to help him.

2. When he got frustrated with himself for not getting something right, I encouraged him by reminding him that he's been through a lot of trauma and healing takes time. I continually reinforced with him that the brain needs time and this is part of the healing

process. I constantly reminded him that he was trying to put all the puzzle pieces together and this was part of the process.

3. I asked him more questions to probe and gain insight into what he was thinking. This helped me identify how his brain was connecting things together and determine which part of the brain his thoughts and actions were originating.

4. Our family would go around the room and say something we for which we were thankful. This helped break difficult moods and lift spirits. This allowed my dad to think about and share something positive.

5. Watch movies together. We rotated who picked the family movie to watch. Everyone learned something!

FAMILY ACTION GUIDE

1. I strongly encourage you to walk in the shoes of your loved one's physical, speech, and occupational therapy sessions, as applicable. This is enlightening, educational, and paramount for continuity of care.

2. Proactively seek out appropriate training, support and coaching. By the time we came across this information, we had been through the first several months of rehabilitation.

3. It is really important to be in continuous contact with all therapists involved in your loved one's care. Talk to the case manager about patient health goals. Determine how the facility and insurance companies determine the goals, progress and baselines. Understanding these measurements is key to advocating for the best care and understanding timelines allowed for certain health progress milestones. Remember that insurance companies will only continue paying for care up to

their maximum limit **and** according to their patient health goal measurements.

4. In determining general activities you can do together, consider what they enjoy doing. When and where possible, design activities around things that make them happy and is within their limitations. Knitting, art, gardening and playing cards are some examples. Foster their excitement.

5. Earlier, I shared ways we helped my dad feel needed. This is important. Identify any simple time appropriate task that your loved one can do that will help them feel productive and needed. If they are able to fold clothes, ask for their help. Laundry, dishes and garbage are just a few examples. When cooking, we gave my mom things to chop, cut or slice. This made her feel like she contributed to our family meals.

6. Find community activities you can do together. Go to public places that aren't time sensitive, such as a zoo, where you can have fun and participate at your schedule without worrying about affecting others.

7. If you suspect elder abuse, I recommend looking into the following resources:

   - Adult Protective Services for your area
   - Social Services for your area
   - Long-Term Care Ombudsman
   - Law Enforcement
   - Your Faith Community
   - Your Health Care Insurance or the facility's care abuse reporting process

8. When the patient is transferred at any point between a skilled nursing facility and other facility or is transferring home, ensure the transferring facility has a thorough, written plan for continuity of care. This can be overlooked in the hustle and

bustle of transfer and discharge. This allows the receiving facility to more easily integrate the patient. When a patient is being transferred home, as the advocate, make sure the case manager and nursing staff work with you to coordinate items needed at home. Items such as bed transfer boards, portable potty chairs, wound care materials, etc... are things that family caregivers can overlook if not discussed prior to discharge.

These are all strategies we found highly effective for my dad's recovery and both of my parents' overall well being. Some of these tips I learned from attending inpatient rehabilitation physical, occupational, and speech therapy sessions and other tips I intuitively thought to do and others I recalled from my kids' elementary school work. You know your loved one better than any practitioner. You know their limits, emotions, goals, and dreams. You have a vested interest in their full recovery. Professionally trained therapists in these areas bring the physiological, psychological, and cognitive training to the table. Together, we are terrific partners in our loved one's healing process.

CHAPTER TEN
Creating a Legacy Today and Tomorrow

"Remember that when you leave this earth, you can take with you nothing that you have received–only what you have given."
~ St. Francis of Assisi

Living our lives with passion and purpose is, I believe, everyone's mission in life. I know following my heart and intuition has served me well and living my life on purpose is such a blessing. Some people live their entire lives not knowing or living their passion. Taking this to another level, some people aren't as fortunate as we were to have my parents alive to document their lives and ask questions important for their legacy.

A legacy is generally thought of as a gift of personal or real property in the event of death, yet I believe legacies are much, much more. Creating a legacy also includes capturing and preserving family stories and history, preserving the integrity of their lives, protecting the family estate and financial planning, learning about the stories and meaning behind their life and belongings loved ones hold near and dear to their heart. Ultimately, our legacies are about what we leave behind, what gifts we have given, what lives and hearts we have touched, who we have served and be who we came here to be. This chapter is about how we defined and preserved our family legacy during this journey and specific tips you can use today to add to your legacy. Perhaps one of these ideas will resonate with you.

Personal Property/Belongings

Most people don't think to ask about most belongings until it's too late and they are going through the house with other family members determining what they want to keep; all while grieving the loss of their loved one. In my experience observing how people can behave after funerals, right after a loved one passes away isn't necessarily the best time to make decisions about what to keep or not as decisions can often be made from a place of emotion and attachment. The result is you can end up with a lot more 'stuff' than you need. You can also end up with unnecessary family strife.

I felt so incredibly fortunate to have a mother who knew my dad so well that it seemed she sometimes knew him better than he knew himself. There wasn't one single item we showed my mom that she couldn't recite the entire story and history behind it. This fascinated me and warmed my heart that she had all of this history.

Therefore, my objective was to capture and share her knowledge with the rest of us! Towards that end, we learned so much about things. For example, we learned that a cloth doily found among old ragged sheets and blankets belonged to my great, great grandmother. No one would have known this story had we not asked.

I learned that a particular knife set I'd always remembered seeing in our kitchen drawers growing up was a wedding gift for my parents. Knowing this just turned an everyday knife set into a family heirloom, we will definitely keep this in the family. Knowing the history behind just about everything now helps me make better decisions about their things moving forward. I'm so glad we cleaned and downsized their home while they were still alive so we could draw out these stories and learn more about their lives together and our ancestors. In the process I learned while some things are sentimental for my parents, they likely won't mean much for us and will likely be donated. Other things we will treasure because we have a greater appreciation for these stories.

Family History Preservation

I believe part of creating a legacy is about preserving your loved one's most valuable asset; learning about life through their stories, hopes, and dreams. This is why we began journaling their stories, insights, and memories about their lives growing up.

I learned a lot about my dad in the ensuing months and years following his accident. Some things I could have lived without knowing were his choices about what to save, his odd sense of humor, his emotional distance, his impulse to please and help others to the detriment of himself and family, and his inconsistency in walking the talk with his financial beliefs. More importantly, there were many things I admired about my dad, such as he always provided for us and took his responsibilities seriously. He believed in education and lifelong learning. He proudly served his country for twenty years in the military. He sacrificed some of his dreams for the sake of the family. He always made me feel safe and protected. They had been through so much and he was always, always by my mom's side. Now, my mom was by his side in his greatest time of need.

Hopes, Dreams and Everything in Between

One of the most powerful things I did in all of my care giving was help my parents document their hopes and dreams, fears, lessons learned and traditions they cherished. Through this experience, I learned so much about my dad. I felt a strong innate need to help my dad find his power and healing through his stories. I wanted to preserve our family history and I wanted to help my parents feel complete when they decided to leave this physical realm. I helped my dad, who was always in his head, express his heartfelt feelings. I learned that by asking him questions I helped him feel and heal while documenting his life.

I gained a whole new perspective into his personality. The most valuable advice my dad received when he was young was from his father. His father taught him it's not what you say but how you say things that matter most. My dad considered life's greatest gift the inalienable rights of life, liberty, and the pursuit of happiness. I learned my dad had never been on a real vacation and he wanted to go to Yellowstone. His favorite song was: "Man in My Little Girl's Life." If he could have only kept one family photo, he would keep "the" family picture with him, my mom, my sister, and me. The people that made the greatest impact on his life included the Tooth Fairy, Santa Clause, his mom and dad, his Grandpa Eulin, Professor Smith, his director of music in High School, and Chaplain Johnson from Wright-Patterson Air Force Base.

Professionally, my dad felt most valued and trusted during a Temporary Duty Yonder (TDY)[11] while in the USAF.[12] With a lump in his throat, he told me he was the 22nd USAF person in Iceland and had top clearance. He had access to anything he needed. If he could have a do over with his career choice, he would have gone into education and been a teacher. His favorite Christmas carol was "The Little Drummer Boy." My dad expressed vulnerability when sharing with me the one time he saw his father cry and what he learned from this experience. These are just some of the things I learned about my dad through this process. I feel fortunate to have learned so much about the man behind the title 'dad' and how his past impacted his decisions and how he raised us.

Sometimes, when my dad and I were alone together in the car going from appointment to appointment, he opened up and shared some of his innermost feelings. I noticed that the night before when he would respond to questions I asked about his life (and I captured responses in writing), he would recall the question and want to talk further about it. What I learned about some of my dad's innermost fears, dreams, and regrets was just how vulnerable, 'broken', and sad he had been. I felt surprised that he would speak from his heart so openly with me. I think he felt safe and trusted me to share his deepest feelings with me. A part of me felt additional burdens with information he shared and these are things I will take with me to my grave, but if we are to really learn about someone, we should learn about the whole person.

I thanked him for sharing with me and expressed my gratitude for raising us. I reaffirmed he was a great father. I learned my dad was actually a man, a human being separate from being my dad. There was a lot about him I didn't really know until now and I was grateful to have a different perspective about my dad.

My mom, too, began to share some of her innermost fears and deep, damaging experiences from her childhood. These conversations typically happened when we drove places together. I gained a deeper appreciation and understanding for her as a person. I felt immense sadness and anger for what she endured and, with my maternal

---

[11] Otherwise called a temporary duty assignment.
[12] United States Air Force

instinct, wanted so much to take her pain away. I gained an appreciation for my mom's incredible strength and knowledge of minute details of their life.

Through these valuable insights, I was able to put many of my own puzzle pieces together about why my childhood was the way it was, why they were the way they were, and coping mechanisms they used throughout their lives. This is one of the many reasons why creating a written legacy is so important; you may realize things about yourself you never knew before or recognized in yourself. I felt profound compassion and love for my parents. This was a gift and helped us heal in our own way.

Reigniting Family Tradition

I found so much value in this process, I was inspired to resume my own family tradition of writing my kids annual letters about the year, key milestones we experienced, the things I was most proud of that year. I included a few key things they wrote, made, or did that year. I sealed up the envelopes, labeled them for the year, and put instructions for the kids to open their envelopes when I decided to give it to them. Somewhere along the line life became too busy and I didn't make time for this anymore or perhaps wrongly thought the kids were too old. Given everything I've learned about my parents and reflecting as a parent myself, I feel one of the greatest gifts we can give our children other than values, core beliefs and life skills to become responsible adults one day is our heartfelt feelings of love and pride. With tearful eyes and a smile from ear to ear, I love recalling favorite childhood memories and our hopes and dreams for them. I can't imagine how long I would probably still be crying had I had something like this from my parents. Especially now, as a parent myself, knowing and feeling the immense, unconditional love from my parents and for my children, this will make a profound impact on my peace of mind and strengthen our relationships even more.

Legal, Financial and Medical Affairs

An equally important aspect of one's legacy is ensuring all legal, medical, and financial affairs are in order. Based on an unrelated surgery in 2005, my dad spent quality time putting everything together we needed. My dad documented his life, including website user names and passwords, what associations he belonged to and their contact information, what life insurance policies he had where for him and my mom and their account numbers and company contact information. He documented his brokerage, bank and credit card accounts, and account numbers, information about their homes. Additionally, he documented his life chronology, including timelines for all his addresses from birth to present; including his employer history, pension information, years worked, and salary history. He even documented all the places he was stationed while in the military. My dad was prepared for anything and now I was prepared. Having a complete life history was one of the best things he ever did aside from having my sister and me.

Having these documents was like winning the lottery when I needed to open it. It probably felt like winning the lottery because everything was together in one, tight, neat package. This proved invaluable for many reasons, including working with his memory recall. During hospital stays, I shared this information with his occupational and speech therapists, which helped determine his brain and memory patterns, decipher fact from fiction, and aid in figuring out how he was putting his 'brain puzzle' together.

On the topic of estate planning, if you don't already have a Durable or Medical Power of Attorney (POA), you need to run somewhere and get this done *today*. Had my mother been dead at the time of my dad's accident, I would have had a much, much harder time with things. Also, in my experience, you can grant someone a blanket POA to take affect whenever they deem appropriate or you can make the POA effective in the event you become incapacitated. In which case, mortgage companies, banks, employers and the like will require documented proof of incapacity, along with the POA document to be valid. It can take time to get this proof and be able to do what you need to do. I also learned some banks use their own guidelines about what documentation they will accept. With a properly executed durable POA that was good enough for all things big and small, one bank in particular required very specific wording and said it wasn't good enough. Wow. The US Government, mortgage companies and most banks accepted this documentation, yet one bank wouldn't. These are just some of the challenges POAs deal with. We strongly suggest you do your research and seek legal counsel when creating or updating a POA and other medical/estate documents.

I implore you to document your life history and get estate planning in order. Do it today. Married, single, kids, no kids, homes, no homes, it doesn't matter. You have a responsibility document your wishes, decide ahead of time who you want to act on your behalf either as a medical power of attorney or general power of attorney. Do you want doctors to save your life at all costs, even if it means living in a persistent, vegetative state? Do you want your closest relative/next of kin to make decisions for you? In what circumstances do you want others to make decisions for you? Do you trust they will act in your best interests?

In this chapter, I weaved things I did well and the things I recommend everyone do from documenting history and sharing stories to legal matters important yet less commonly discussed. I recommend doing these things NOW before you are faced with family members or yourself needing to act quickly. I preface information contained herein with a disclaimer that you should consult an attorney, CPA, or other professional for advice on how to proceed with your particular situation.

FAMILY ACTION GUIDE

1. Get or update your will. Depending on your situation, you may want to get a trust. My dad completed his POA (as part of the envelope noted above) using a wills and trusts software package. It served us well except for that one darn bank. Be sure to ask designated individuals if they are willing to serve in said role before finalizing any POA's, wills and/or trusts. NOTE: Please seek legal advice for any questions pertaining to your specific situation.

2. Tell your loved ones today where you keep all legal documentation.

3. Create your personal and family legacy by documenting and sharing stories. Ask your loved ones questions to draw out information you may not know. Here are some life categories to get you thinking about:

   a. Biographical information and family information. This includes extended family going back as many generations as they can remember.

   b. List of favorite things. Everybody has a favorite book, song, movie, food, drink, color, clothes, and gifts. The list goes on. Do they have favorite memories of pets?

   c. Positive and negative influences; both past and present.

   d. Favorite historical stories

   e. Everything childhood and family. Who, what, when, where, why and how? Include religion and/or spiritual beliefs, traditions and childhood and family activities.

   f. Education and lifelong learning. Who, what, when, where, why and how.

   g. Career/Job. Why the career they chose? Best boss? Worst boss? Best lesson? What about their first job?

   h. Who inspires them or who has inspired them the most and why?

   i. Relationships. This could include family, spouse, partner, friends, siblings and/or any role they have in life. Include past and present. Any regrets? Funniest moments? Most embarrassing moment? It's important to know that it's natural to have some life regrets. To the extent possible, let it go. It's in the past. There is nothing you can do about it.

j. Favorite vacations and hobbies.

k. What are they most grateful for? What is the best advice you have ever received? What is their proudest moment to date?

We have no promise of tomorrow. If you suddenly died, would your family know how you felt, what you were most proud of, who influenced you the most and why, or what your favorite traditions were growing up? Is it clear who has legal authority to act on your behalf? There are so many aspects to creating a legacy. Practical matters such as ensuring loved ones are protected and care received is according to expressed wishes are important. Equally important is ensuring stories are shared so they can live on for generations to come. This is time that must be invested.

"No one wants to die. Even people who want to go to heaven don't want to die to get there. And yet death is the destination we all share. No one has ever escaped it. And that is as it should be, because Death is very likely the single best invention of Life. It is Life's change agent. It clears out the old to make way for the new. Right now the new is you, but someday not too long from now, you will gradually become the old and be cleared away. Sorry to be so dramatic, but it is quite true. Your time is limited; so don't waste it living someone else's life. Don't be trapped by dogma —which is living with the results of other people's thinking. Don't let the noise of others' opinions drown out your own inner voice. And most important, have the courage to follow your heart and intuition. They somehow already know what you truly want to become. Everything else is secondary."

~ Steve Jobs

CHAPTER ELEVEN
Many Paths to Wellness

"We are energy beings connected to one another through the consciousness of our right hemispheres as one human family. And right here, right now we are brothers and sisters, here to make the world a better place. And in this moment, we are whole, we are perfect, and we are beautiful."

~ Jill Bolte Taylor

The path to wellness can take many approaches. While they may not relate to everyone, these strategies worked for our family. I have practiced many such strategies, including affirmations, prayer, visualizations, meditation, hypnotherapy, tuning forks, thought field therapy, coaching, and Reiki (an ancient energetic healing technique) over the last decade into my life with wild success.

This chapter addresses how I encouraged my parents wellness, including reaffirming their belief that we have the power to do and accomplish anything we put our minds to. I'll describe the powerful spirit residing in my dad and share examples of how determination and power manifested in our daily lives. We saw miracle after miracle with my father's health that demonstrated this power. I also address the amazing power and influence my dogs had on their health. I'll end with a family action guide with specific tips you can incorporate into your life for healing and peace.

Reiki and Resolve

During one night of my dad's hospitalizations, around 1:00 am, everyone left for quick nap breaks while my mom and I remained at the hospital with my dad. The hospital sent up their priest to pray with us and for my dad. After each of my dad's brain surgeries, I gave my dad Reiki. Reiki is a form of therapy that uses simple, hands-on, no-

149

touch, and visualization techniques, to improve the flow of life energy in someone. It involves using our hands to move universal life energy through the body or release. I was able to feel where his energy was blocked and work to release it. I gave my dad Reiki (as I often did), said silent affirmations and prayers, and talked to him as if he could hear and understand us, as I knew he could. At 4:30 am, the priest left his room. At 4:45 am, my mom and I left for home. I needed rest and desperately needed to get home before rush hour started. The last thing we needed was another family car accident. At 5:10 am, my sister returned to the hospital and at 5:15 am he opened his eyes, his vitals returned to normal, and a doctor came and removed his breathing tube.

He was breathing on his own! The first thing he did was ask Felicity for coffee. The second thing he did was tell Felicity that pain is okay because it means you are alive. Simultaneously, as my mom and I lay our heads on our pillows, my sister called and my dad wanted to talk to us. While on the phone, my dad said, "Hello beautiful" to my mom. I think this meant more to her than he will ever know. He was talking completely normal—at pre-accident levels and for the next 24-hours, he talked and talked and talked and talked and talked. He definitely made up for lost time. When I say he was talking, I mean he was completely lucid, talking in complete sentences and remembering pre-accident events. We thoroughly enjoyed having him 'back' that day. It was short lived. After 24-hours, he returned to yet a new, declining functioning baseline than he had before. We cherished those 24-hours.

Canines Natural Healing Senses

My mom is stronger than I thought she was; yet, she was suffering inside a lot more than she let on. I learned I needed to have a close pulse on my mom's emotional, mental, and physical state as she allowed herself to get overwhelmed or sick and wouldn't say anything so as to not 'bother' me. I think she put herself on the backburner. As was typical for my mom, she gave light to the fact she put my dad's recovery ahead of her own well-being. I learned, though, to pay close attention to the signals my dogs gave when something was wrong with her. For example, they would sniff her legs and continue sniffing, then come to me and whine or bark and go back and sniff some more.

They were pretty insistent about it. I would ask my mom if everything was okay and she would say, "Yeah, I'm fine." I pulled up her leg pants to find her legs swollen, extremely red, and infected. I took her to the doctor and he sent us to the hospital where she was admitted for congestive heart failure, cellulites, and worsening kidney failure. Had my dogs not alerted me, I probably would have continued focusing only on my dad. Note that my dogs had no formal guide dog training. This makes every experience with our dogs that much more meaningful.

Another one of our dogs, also with no special training, saved my dad's life multiple times by alerting me when he was having a seizure and was unresponsive or alerted me when his blood sugar was extremely low. When my mom had cancer, both our dogs favored that area of the body. When my dogs favored a certain area of my body, I went to the doctor and was diagnosed with cancer for a third time. I don't know who saved whom but I know dogs have remarkable senses. There are so many stories about our canine and feline family that it could be another book entirely.

The Power of Music and Hypnosis

Music is a universal language. Music and songs can speak to the heart in powerful ways. I believe music is to words like video is to words. It has the power to touch your soul on a deep level. We've always been a music family. All genres are fair game.

Music and hypnosis together can also be a powerful healing tool. Being a Certified Hypnotherapist, I blended hypnosis and music for my parents' healing. Hypnosis speaks to the subconscious mind; that part of you that knows the truth of who you really are. Our conscious mind gets in the way of change through analysis, ego, criticism, and negative internal dialog that can wreck havoc on you body and efforts to heal. I blended music and hypnotherapy as a path to wellness.

A key thing I did was make custom music selections for my parents and put this music compilation on an iPod and CD's. Felicity loves music as much as I do and she, too, put song compilations together for them. Some of the music was upbeat and part of their respective favorite collections, others were meditations I inserted to promote healing, and others were heartfelt songs; many of which were songs I felt about them and wanted them to know. This dedication compilation would play with their headsets as they drifted off to sleep and I had my dad's music on every time he napped, slept, recovered from surgery, and when he was unconscious. Never underestimate the power of music. One profound experience I had with my dad occurred one day when he was resting comfortably in his hospital bed, when I put his headphones on and played George Straits's song, "I saw God today."

As the song played, tears began to stream from my dad's face. I've never seen my dad cry. I looked at where he was in the song and later listened to the song again with that point in mind and started crying myself. I felt a surge of emotions swirling around my body. I tingled all over. I grieved for the loss of my dad before he would die. I grieved for the immense sadness and trapped feelings he must have felt at the time. I grieved for the fear he may have experienced about the dying process and his questioning what would really happen to him at and after death.

One night as my mom was playing, "I Want to Hold Your Hand" by the Beatles, I saw her sway from side to side at the edge of their bed, lay down and reach over to hold my dad's hand, and go to sleep. This warmed my heart feeling we picked just the right songs for them.

Among my parent's respective music selections were hypnosis CD's with healing affirmations. These are CD's I use with clients and use myself. Tarra, my spiritual mentor for many years, recommended I do hypnosis with my dad with my own voice live and in person. The sound of my voice would help them connect and grab on to this healing modality. The iPod was for them to listen to when I wasn't there. My dad would never admit that hypnosis, visualizations, or affirmations worked, but all be darned if he listened to them ever so intently. Several times, as nurses, therapists, or doctors were entering the room, I tried taking the headphones off and he would open his eyes and with his left hand trying to stop me. I was floored. My heart smiled inside, feeling I was doing the right things with him. While I visited my dad in the hospital and even at home in the evenings as he lay to sleep, I would hold his hand or touch his arm and speak healing and positive sayings and affirmations. I led his subconscious mind through visualization exercises designed to clear out negativity, stress and disease, and feel at peace. While my dad rarely said this helped him, his energy and facial expressions told me it did.

The Power of Prayer

Another key healing component was prayer. I had special prayers for my parents that helped us detach physically from one another while sending them positive, healing thoughts energetically. I invoked and affirmed the powerful presence of God, Ascended Masters, Archangels and Angels to guide me. They have done a terrific job up to this point and much of the credit for what I did right goes to them. I was intuitive and in tune enough to listen and take action. This time to and for myself helped me clear negative energy, reconnect and affirm we were all being supported, thus allowing for a more restful night's sleep.

When I talk about detaching from my parents' physically, I mean that, because we were so close, sometimes I would feel heaviness in my legs, lungs, heart, shoulders, and other areas of my body where they were carrying aches and pains. Sometimes, I felt so open energetically that they would draw from my light and energy to help them get through the day. That's all well and good except it took its toll on me. Mind you, this isn't something that I believe people do consciously. Because I was aware of it, I was able to clear all of these little attachments and stand separate from my parents. I found this immensely helpful. Here are some prayers I used and found immediately beneficial.

One such prayer I reference above is:

Dearest God, Great Spirit, and all Angels and Guides, please fill my parents with peace, love and light; releasing all fears, doubts, and worry. Please help break down any and all fears and barriers so when it is their time, they may return home to you in peace, love, and light. Please help me and our family be filled with love and laughter in our everyday lives and see the positive side of everything. Help us become closer as a family and be compassionate, patient, kind, and respectful as possible and serve as a positive support system for one another. Help my parents know, feel, and believe in your presence and have confidence that their wishes will be carried out. Please give me the strength, courage, love, energy, and light to serve and help them and serve as a beacon of light for my family through this transition. Help us say and do whatever necessary to be complete and at peace with each other. Please minimize suffering for all and in all ways. Guide me towards right actions in all aspects of this situation. Thank you for the amazing patience, compassion, love, trust, wisdom, and tolerance I have now. Help me maintain a full perspective on this and all situations. Help and guide us all towards our souls' purpose and let the learning in this situation be revealed and its potential maximized for all. Help all of us let go and detach from any specific outcome, be open, and receive the lessons my father is teaching us all. Help him feel good about being our master teacher and help my parents feel good about their life, legacy, and their eventual transition home. Thank you for your favor. Amen

Another prayer is:

Dear God and Archangel Raphael, thank you for reigniting my passion for life. Thank you for helping me enjoy each moment and face any challenges with grace and excitement. Please guide me to be strong, to speak my truth, and to stand up for myself when necessary. Infuse the truth of my being throughout every cell in my body. Thank you for giving me the energy and perseverance to meet my responsibilities and still stay true to myself. Amen.

A popular prayer I used is: "The light of God surrounds me. The love of God enfolds me. The power of God protects me. The presence of God watches over me. Wherever I am, God is."[13]

Another prayer I said is:

Great Spirit, please come to me now. Please clear this room and home of all low energy and help us all be happy, calm, patient, and compassionate. Thank you for protecting all who enter here and may all involved in our care be guided to always do the right thing. Amen.

Some affirmations I found helpful included:

I am at peace in this moment. I only think about the one thing I'm doing. I am having peaceful thoughts. I live in an abundant universe: I choose to think about what I have and I will be fine. The universe will and does provide everything I need.

I am grateful for everyone God sends to my path and I know that as a co creator, it is up to me to resonate with the high, loving energy of intention and send him or her a silent blessing and thank you.

I let go and let God.

I live in a universe that attracts healing. I choose thoughts that make me feel good, and this will help me uplift those in need.

I attract detachment. I attract generosity to the world with my abundance.

I give thanks for healing emerald green healing light now, restoring complete health and balance. I give thanks for my open mind,

---

[13] James Dillet Freeman

emotions, and spirit to Divine healing energy, allowing me to be a perfect conduit for healing in all ways.

I am grateful now for my mind's ability to help me relax, trust, and let go. I give thanks for enjoying a wonderful night's sleep. I now feel safe and loved.

Archangel Raphael, please come to me now and comfort my mind and soothe my heart. I am willing to give you and God all of my cares and worries if you will please assist me in letting them go. Help me to know that I am safe in all ways. Thank you for shifting my thoughts to peace.

Feel free to use any or all of these prayers and affirmations as you feel guided to or change them up a bit to meet your specific needs. I have dozens of pages full of prayers, affirmations, and visualization exercises for many situations. If you have other prayers or exercises on this or related topics, I'd love to hear about them and how they have helped you. For more information about Angels and Archangels, I recommend checking out Doreen Virtue at www.angeltherapy.com and/or Sunny Dawn Johnston at www.sunnydawnjohnston.com.

Essential Oils, Tuning Forks and Space Clearing

I believe in and fully blend alternative medicine with western medicine. I believe both are needed at times. My mom and I used essential oils. My great aunt, Mary Ellen, was quick to share remedies for a myriad of things. I used tuning forks, sound therapy, and space clearing techniques such as saging rooms and clapping around doors, windows or any area of our home where energy felt stagnant or I wanted to increase the positive flow in that area. I maximized our home energy with feng shui wherever we could. I took both my parents for holographic repatterning sessions at different stages in their recovery. For my skeptical dad, the experience freed him to share things with me that he probably would not have been inspired to share had he not experienced releases through this healing modality.

As you can see, I didn't leave much to chance. I share in this chapter quite a few tools I incorporated into our lives. Many of these were things I used in my life before late 2009 and others I learned about and used along the way. Some things helped more than others and, collectively, our faith in God carried us through.

FAMILY ACTION GUIDE

1. To the extent appropriate to your faith and beliefs, integrate these or any other practices into your daily life.

2. Seek out at least one alternative healing modality; one that resonates with you. Perhaps it was an idea from this chapter. Perhaps it's something else. There is no right or wrong answer or method.

3. Have daily prayers, affirmations and/or visualization exercises as part of your life success tool kit. Visit my website at www.tandyelisala.com for free resources and information on related products and services to aid in your personal, professional and spiritual development.

CHAPTER TWELVE
Life Must Go On

"Life is a succession of lessons which must be lived to be understood".

~ *Ralph Waldo Emerson*

This journey has profoundly changed me in so many ways. I feel an expanded capacity for compassion. We've all healed in ways we needed to, grown in ways we couldn't have imagined, and created even stronger bonds of love. I've always felt our family was close, but I feel our family has grown so much more through the challenges, trials, and tribulations in ways I didn't think possible. One of the questions I am asked most often is how on earth did I get through all of this. Well, here's *what I know for sure*:

1. Now, more than ever, I live consistently and in alignment with my values and beliefs. When I live consistent with my passion, life purpose, and values, things are easier, everything is clearer and I am open to receiving the lessons in all experiences. Making time and getting results seems almost effortless. I truly 'got' that when we aren't moving in alignment with spirit, our values, and beliefs, everything becomes a struggle and disease manifests somehow and somewhere in our lives or in our physical bodies.

2. I would have waves of living my truth of who I know I am over the years and feel that I am now completely detached from my title, position, or other labels we put on ourselves. I know, feel, and believe I made the right decisions for my growth. There were so many people who tried telling me that it's not my responsibility to take care of my parents, or say they couldn't do what I did. Some people advised me to just put them in a home and visit when you can. I knew, felt, and believed this wasn't the right solution for our situation. When the time came

that their level of care needed exceeded our abilities, we moved them where they needed to be in their final days. If the roles were reversed, I certainly wouldn't want to be alone in a 'home' with no family.

3. I drew from life experiences to help me grow. I am a better mother, daughter, sister, friend, leader, and person as a result of increased compassion and enhanced space available for things anew than I was. All of my experiences carry over and impact how I lead my teams, raise my children, spend my time, and honor myself.

4. My spiritual beliefs without question served me well through my darkest hours. I believe that when our physical body dies, our soul lives on. When my grandmother died in 2002, I mourned her loss. I cried knowing I would never hug her again, see her smile, hear her laugh, or eat her cooking. I had a deep knowing she would watch over us, be there for us, and help us in ways she couldn't in the physical realm. I had comfort in knowing that my relationship with my parents would and will be just as strong, if not stronger after death because, they, too, would help and protect us. My beliefs about death and dying and what happens after death brought me comfort and joy. I knew that no matter what happened, we are 'soul' family.

5. My faith and belief that our Heavenly Father will guide me through all things brings immense tearful joy every day. I believe if we put our worries in God's hands and truly listen to guidance, He will pave the way through anything. He carries us, wipes our tears, listens to our prayers, and always guides us in the right direction at the right time.

6. I knew, felt, and believed in the power of the mind. My dad is a prime example of the power of our minds to heal. I have healed myself from a hernia, helped shrink cancer, helped clients overcome a variety of things and through my spiritual

journey, I always knew the power of our minds could do literally anything we put our minds to. Although I fell off the cart, so to speak, in recent years, this experience has reinforced my belief in something greater than ourselves and in the power we all have inside to change our lives.

7. I drew from my immense strength. I've always been a strong person. This buffer I built over the years helped me navigate through all the craziness, tragedy, senseless, hopelessness, and anger and turn tragedy into inspiration, make sense of the senseless, turn helplessness into hope and anger into peace.

8. Death is a natural part of life. We all have to bury our parents at some point in our lives. My sister is the only person in the entire world who understood what we were going through. The love. The loss. The grief. The memories. In many respects, however, Felicity and I would grieve different people as each of our relationships with our parents was different. The same holds true for my children, when the time comes, at least six decades from now, when they bury me. They will only have each other. Yes, they will have their own families, and that's important. The bond between siblings though; there is nothing like it.

I think Maya Angelou sums it up best:

"I've learned that no matter what happens, or how bad it seems today, life does go on, and it will be better tomorrow. I've learned that you can tell a lot about a person by the way he/she handles these three things: a rainy day, lost luggage, and tangled Christmas tree lights. I've learned that regardless of your relationship with your parents, you'll miss them when they're gone from your life. I've learned that making a "living" is not the same thing as making a "life." I've learned that life sometimes gives you a second chance. I've learned that you shouldn't go through life with a catcher's mitt on both hands; you need to be able to throw something back. I've learned that whenever I decide something with an open heart, I usually make the right decision. I've learned that even when I have pains, I don't have to be one. I've learned that every day, you should reach out and touch someone. People love a warm hug, or just a friendly pat on the back. I've learned that I still have a lot to learn. I've learned that people will forget what you said, people will forget what you did, but people will never forget how you made them feel."

Here we are towards the end of this care giving journey. There are moments of impact that turn our lives upside down. How we choose to handle these moments is up to us. It takes courage to do the right thing at the right time and for the right reasons. I feel grateful to have been guided to do just that.

Yes, there are moments of impact that turn our lives upside down. May we all be filled with grace, courage, and peace to lovingly handle these moments. It is through these moments of impact we learn more about ourselves and others than we ever thought possible.

One of Amanda's favorite quotes is *Ernest Hemingway's*: "Courage is grace under pressure." Indeed, it is. Courage is also vulnerability. Rather, courage requires vulnerability. There is something very vulnerable about the prospect of dying.

CHAPTER THIRTEEN
Circle Of Life ~ Circle Of Love: The Last Breath

"Our death is not an end if we can live on in our children and the younger generation. For they are us, our bodies are only wilted leaves on the tree of live."

~ Albert Einstein

Remember, "What lies behind us and what lies before us are tiny matters compared to what lies within us."

~ Ralph Waldo Emerson

I started this book by saying that absolutely nothing prepared me for this care giving journey. My initial book ending shared how we were doing as of the date of publication. With all the hustle and bustle, I delayed getting my final draft to the editor. May 2, 2012, I realized why. Tragedy creates purpose...at least it did for me. This chapter needed to be added to complete this book.

Our next D-Day started April 30, 2012. This is the day Amanda took my mom to the doctor's office because her bronchitis wasn't responding to antibiotics. In the days leading to this day, I asked her if she wanted to go to the doctor, urgent care, or the ER. She affirmed she wanted to stay home. I started hearing chest noises from her I've never heard before. Being an asthmatic myself, I was all too familiar with troubling asthmatic sounds. These sounds were different. With every breath she took, it sounded like rattling and crackling. I repeatedly asked her if she wanted to go get help. She was adamant that she wanted to stay home. In prior discussions with my parents, they both said they wanted to die at home. This is part of the reason we took on this responsibility: to help them live and die with dignity together.

During the month of April 2012, she went to the doctor at least once weekly; sometimes every two to three days to check on her bronchitis and legs. Amanda took her to the ER twice. Doctors released my mother at her request. I observed that she spent the vast majority of days sleeping. She started eating less. Her skin was thinning and she started bruising easily. It seemed like anything touching her arms or legs became blistery. Her nail beds became brittle and fluctuated colors. Her lips were turning purplish/bluish. Then her feet, ankles, and legs from the knee down were purple.

I think somehow I knew. I would listen to her breathing from my room and my heart sunk into my stomach feeling like she was going to die any day. I was angry thinking that she would be the first parent to die. My dad was driving her crazy (her words) and I wanted her to have some happiness. This wasn't in the cards and it's about what she wanted or at least what her body and soul was ready for.

April 30, 2012, Amanda took my mom to the doctor kicking and screaming. Immediately after laying eyes on my mom, the doctor's office called for an ambulance. She tried negotiating, asking, "How about we don't go to the hospital and do home healthcare instead?" Amanda bent down and told my mom...her grandma...that she knew she was scared and felt like she may not come home, yet she needed to be at the hospital right now. My mom affirmed she understood Amanda. She still wasn't happy about it, though.

Upon admission, doctors confirmed a pneumonia diagnosis. With her COPD, congestive heart failure, asthma, diabetes, severe stage four kidney failure, and, for the last month, large blistering wounds accompanying severe leg swelling. She was in bad shape.

May 1, 2012, when my daughter Sarah and I visited my mom, she looked different to me. She appeared resigned, sullen, and quiet. Usually when she is in hospitals, she is sad, yet has a long list of things to bring from home. This time, she had two things on her list: her boot (she suffered a broken ankle a month prior) and her Sudoku book. I repeatedly asked if there was anything else she wanted and she shook her head no. As Sarah lay across her grandma's hospital bed, my mom started caressing Sarah's hair. As we left, my mom asked Sarah to do a quick dance and sing something for her. You see, Sarah has always been the dramatic one who loves to dance and be the center of attention and the center of laughter in our home. Her bubbly personality and contagious love for life brought joy to my parents.

Sarah did a little dance twirl thing and my mom smiled and said, "Thank you, Sarah. I love you." In a high-pitched voice, Sarah said "I love you, too, Grandma" and gave her a hug. I gave my mom a hug and said, as I always did, "I love you, Mom. Grandpa and Steven will be by later with your boot and Sudoku book." She replied, "I love you more" to which I replied, "I love *you* more." As I said that, we were in the hallway leaving her room and, as I turned back, I could see her smiling. This was the last time I would hug her and feel her embrace, see her beautiful smile and feel her unwavering love beaming from every ounce of her physical being. As we walked down the hall to the elevator, I was fighting back the tears. This was the second time in my life my mom said, "I love you more."

Around 10:00 pm, May 1, I received a call from my mom's nurse saying that she went into cardiac arrest and she was unable to breathe on her own. They put her on a ventilator and moved her to Intensive Care. They wanted me to be aware of her changing condition. Around midnight, I received a call from her doctor providing updates. Around 2:00 am, I received another call from the doctor explaining her condition and what it may mean. We discussed options and touched base a few hours later. I called Felicity at some point between the doctor calls. When I last talked to the doctor (and nurse), they said she was stable (if having a machine breathe for you is stable) and the next few days would be telling. There was absolutely zero reason why my dad couldn't proceed with gallbladder surgery the next day. Yep, my dad was stable and feeling well enough to have gallbladder surgery. He was in a lot of pain. I explained this to my mom's medical team and they said not to worry.

As luck would have it, Amanda had jury duty. She was selected as a juror for a trial starting May 2. Amanda felt compelled to visit my mom early in the morning before leaving across town for jury duty. Thank God she did.

Early May 2, 2012, as Amanda was getting up, I told her what happened and asked her for feedback on whether I should tell my dad or leave it alone so he wouldn't worry during surgery and give him her health update afterwards. She affirmed what I was thinking: I needed to tell my dad what was going on with his wife of forty-four years. As my dad was getting ready to go to a different hospital. I sat him down and explained the events of the previous night. He affirmed he wanted to proceed with surgery. *At least I gave him the choice*, I thought. I took my dad to one hospital while Amanda visited my mom at another hospital. As I completed pre-op details with my dad's nurse, Amanda calls. She is crying and had a panic in her voice I'd never heard before. She quivered, "You need to get down here right now, Mom. Like, you don't understand. You need to be here now!" My mom's blood pressure was around 40/25. I told Amanda to tell my mom that she needs to hold on until her babies get there. As Amanda told her this, my mom's blood pressure teetered around 70/50.

I started shaking and I could feel my pulse beating hard and my blood pressure rising. Leaning up against the counter in the next room to maintain balance, I immediately called Felicity and told her she needed to leave work and get to the hospital immediately. I then called my dear friend, Rose. I asked if she was able to come relieve me and take care of my dad and ensure he gets home okay and explained what was going on with my mom. Thank goodness she was able to help. I knew I needed to be with my mom, yet someone had to be there to take my dad home. I am so thankful Rose came to my aid when I needed it most. Rose is one of the most thoughtful, caring and generous people I have the pleasure of calling my friend. I then called Steven out of school citing a family emergency and said he needed to walk home immediately. Sarah was home and I told her to get her brother and meet at my dad's hospital, pick me up outside, and we would jet over to my mom's hospital.

Leaving my dad's belongings with the nurse, I kissed my dad, told him what was happening, and, with a sad face, he said, "Tell her I love her and I will see her for our 45th wedding anniversary dance." He then muttered, "Wouldn't that be funny if both of us died today?" I started crying and told him that wasn't funny. My heart skipped a few beats when he mentioned their 45th wedding anniversary as that was only 1 ½ months away! I could only think of one thing at a time right now and that was my mom.

We all seemed to arrive within five minutes of each other. Amanda called the juror's office, explaining why she wouldn't be there. As soon as Amanda arrived that morning, the hospice nurse was waiting for family to arrive and told Amanda we needed to discuss hospice options, as it appeared my mom only had a few days left to live. Between 8:00 am and 9:00 am, my mom's condition worsened. Hospice was no longer an option. Upon arrival, I was met with a nurse in my mom's room. The nurse was clear with me that my mom would die today and she would die in this room, Room # 12. It was a far cry from home, where she wanted to die. Given her medical condition, we reconciled that she was where she needed to be.

Felicity, Amanda, Sarah, Steven, and I stood around her bed. I noticed that all of us were touching her in some way. Over the next 5 ½ hours, we all watched her condition deteriorate. I did notice, however, that when we would get up close to her head and talk to her, her vitals improved...for a few moments. During this time, we cried, we sang, we prayed, and we talked to her as we played some of her favorite songs. When we played ABBA's song "Dancing Queen," her left foot moved through the song as if it was her way of dancing. Then, we each sat around her bed, held hands, and went around the room saying what we were thankful and grateful for about her. We did this several times around the room. We told her it was okay to go. The hospital priest came and prayed with us several times. We talked about some of our funny moments with my mom. We'd ask her questions as if she could answer them. We played songs that had messages of love as dedications from us to her. Most songs we played for us all and sang to were songs we put on her iPod. We all talked about memories we had of her over the years. We told jokes. We cried some more.

Amanda and I called her sisters, Robin and Cindy, in Oklahoma. Affirming they wouldn't be able to get here in time, I held the phone up to my mom's ear as Robin talked to her. Robin was able to say what she wanted to say. She was very distraught to say the least. The hospital staff was fabulous about respecting our wishes and leaving us alone (except to give her IV pain medication.). It was a serendipitous moment when we all looked at each other and felt complete. Immediately, my mom's remaining life force energy slowly sucked away. Nurses told us it was close and said to let her know when we were ready to turn off the machine. They said if there was anyone else coming, they needed to come quickly.

I called Rose to get a status on my dad. I thought on the outside chance he was feeling well enough to come visit his wife and say goodbye, they may make it in time. Rose said he was still in recovery. My dad's surgery took longer than expected, as there was a complication. Interesting 'coincidence' that both parents were 'out of it' at the same time. Knowing his condition, Felicity and I touched our mom, looked at each other across the bed, and gave the okay to terminate life support.

With the machine off, we all sat and waited and watched and cried. A few minutes later, she opened her glossy eyes, turned her head asking what was going on. She was weak and we really had to listen closely to hear what she was saying. The nurse came to her bedside and explained what happened and she was dying. Confused and with her eyebrows squinted together, she looked at me and I repeated what happened and gently told her she was dying. I asked her to shake her head if she understood what I was saying. She nodded and looked over at Felicity. Sobbing, Felicity told her it was okay to go and that she would be okay. Mom turned her head back over to me and whispered, "Carmine." I said that Carmine (her cat) would be safe and taken care of. I promised her we would take care of him. She nodded. She then said "Bill." I've never heard my mom refer to our dad by his first name. Without skipping a beat, I asked if she remembered he was scheduled for surgery that day and told her he was in recovery and he would be okay. Her face softened and she leaned into her pillow. While she was conscious, I held back many of my tears because I felt I needed to be the strong one. I suppose I didn't want my mom to see me crying and misinterpret it for being unable to handle things.

In that moment, with a heart-wrenching look on her face crying, Amanda turned to me saying, "I can't do this. I can't be in the room when she dies. I just can't!" I hugged her and told her it was okay. She needed to do what was right for her and Grandma knew she was there. She left the room. As the rest of us continued touching her, we felt temperature changes on her sheen skin. Another five minutes passed and we all continued crying and telling her it was okay to go. When the nurse came back in the room, Steven and Sarah went to the corner of the room and held hands. Amanda returned. Taking over for the nurse, Amanda took a wet washcloth and ever so sweetly and softly caressed her face and wiped her mouth. At her head, Amanda was crying but she, too, was fighting back tears.

In the moments before her death and with everyone by her side, Sarah and Steven joined us as we touched and caressed her. What happened next was almost indescribable. We all felt the moment she left; the moment she died. Weeping sounds abound, I found myself screaming. I screamed at the top of my lungs. Crying and screaming, I felt every ounce of anger; rage, sorrow, love, and relief come out of my screaming mouth. I felt like a part of me was gone. I wanted her life force energy back. I needed my mom. Flashing before my eyes at a screen running across my mind, it seemed like every single memory of us came whipping across my swirling head. I couldn't stop crying. I was inconsolable. Despite Felicity and my kids huddled around me trying to tell me it was okay, I screamed louder. I thought...*It is NOT okay*. As time passed, I continued screaming and, at some point, realized my hands were clutched onto my mom's arm and hand. I held on tighter, like a hiker holding onto the top of a ledge with nothing separating her from the ground way beneath her. Nurses came in and tried to reassure me everything was going to be alright. The priest returned and he, too, tried consoling me. I didn't know what came over me. As I calmed down, I sensed that my kids were beside themselves with fear. They had never seen me like this. I had to pull myself together.

Tears wiped and as I took care of the logistics, everyone in the nurses' station and surrounding rooms looked up to see who the bellowing, out of control person was. Time of death: 3:25 pm. This is what my eyes went to first when reviewing the death certificate form.

Upon reflection, we couldn't have done this better had we planned it. I would say without my immediate reaction, we couldn't have planned her death better, but I needed to release my emotions. I needed to grieve the way my body naturally needed to. All in all, it was perfect. Everyone she loved most in the world was with her. Dad was with her in spirit. The day wouldn't have been so synergistic, beautiful, and peaceful had Dad been there. The energy wouldn't have been the same. Everything just flowed out of us all and worked in concert together, like glowing and inspiring ballerinas dancing across the stage.

Her funeral was lovely. My good friend, Mark, presided over her memorial service. Several months prior, Mark told me one of the things he hated in life was attending funeral services, however, he worked for a wonderful religious science church, Creative Living Fellowship, and talked of continuing his ministry education. When I asked Mark to preside over my mom's service, it was because he was a wonderful friend who I knew would comfort me and keep me grounded and I wanted to stretch him personally and professionally. This was the first time he presided over a memorial service and he did a wonderful job. Felicity put together an absolutely phenomenal slide show celebrating her life. She also had a video of the three of us in the car returning home from a trip to Vegas we took her on five or so years ago. Our mom was dancing in the video as only she would. We ended the service playing this video as it was funny, positive, and her true personality shined through. Afterwards, we hosted dinner at one of her favorite places: Spaghetti Factory. We all had a wonderful evening and felt so much love and support from everyone that day and the week prior as friends rallied to help us in many ways.

In the ensuing days and weeks ahead, my dad would sit in their room and just stare at things. He came close to crying several times. One day, I sat at the end of his bed and asked if he was okay. He replied, "No, I'm not okay. I miss her." He choked up and I put my hand on his knee. He was completely lost. Thankfully, his brother, Riley, came and helped everyone immensely. My dad asked me to clear out Mom's dresser. I did but I had to do things in spurts. For physical and emotional health reasons, I couldn't do everything at once. Fifteen to twenty-minute spurts was about all I could handle.

Fast forward to late July 2012. My dad needed another brain surgery. Yep, *another* surgery. After we agreed no more surgeries, he was absolutely fanatic about wanting the surgery. There were so many things that went awry during the stay; I won't go into details, except to say the hospital staff knowingly had my dad sign surgery consent after

I declined it repeatedly. After so many surgeries, they allowed a man with traumatic brain injury in a coherent moment to sign surgery consent. He didn't even have his glasses on and yet they encouraged him to sign the form. He kept talking about dying during surgery. He asked for my kids to come down so he can talk to them. He gave them advice about life and told them all he loved them. After telling me he had nothing left to say to me, he asked for Felicity. She went, and, let's just say she came out crying and said he better not die now because that was the worst goodbye ever. No advice. No parting words. Bottom line is he had the surgery. It took hours longer than expected. There were several moments in the waiting room when Felicity and I looked up at each other and got teary eyed. We felt something was wrong. My chest felt heavy. The surgeon visited and said everything went fine,but he was still in the operating room awaiting more test results. When completed, he was sewn up and went to recovery.

In recovery, when my dad saw my face, he looked really angry. His arms were restrained to the bed. He kept saying he wanted to go. He looked at the nurse and said he needed to leave as he tried getting his legs over the chrome bedside bars. He told her he was going home now. For a few minutes, I helped the nurse keep him restrained and then I saw his eyes. I thought to myself, *I wonder if he is talking about going home as in dying.* As he continued insisting on going home, I said, "Dad, I know you want to go home. That would be nice, wouldn't it? Right now, you are here and in the hospital recovering from brain surgery. You will go home when it's time." He looked at me with glazed eyes and relented, "How do I leave? How do I get out? How do I get out of here? I don't know how to leave!" I got teary eyed and said, "I know, Dad. It's been a long road and you have endured so much pain. I would want to leave, too. When you are ready, you'll be able to leave." Note that I was vague in my response for a reason. He could interpret this how he wanted. His eyes told a story. His eyes were different, distant, and void and showed he had already left.

We brought him home from the hospital, but he was never the same after that. For almost a month, he was severely confused, withdrawn, and sullen. He slept about twenty hours a day, he didn't eat much, he lost interest in TV, was, once again, unable to control his bladder and bowels, and was generally disoriented. Nearly a month after discharge, my dad was having uncontrollable seizures, which is what took him to the hospital in August. He had periods of unconsciousness. I took him to the ER and they confirmed he had yet another brain bleed and it was quickly putting pressure on the entire left side of his brain. Without surgery, blood would continue pressing against his brain and he would likely aspirate and die. My dad and I both agreed this was it. No more. He said he wasn't opposed to surgery; he was opposed to pain and further degradation afterwards! He was tired of being like this and realized his quality of life greatly diminished.

I can't say enough good things about the hospital (the same hospital where my mom died). Once we agreed hospice and palliative care was the route we wanted, AmericaCare representatives arrived within forty-five minutes. ER moved us to a private, more dignified room with a door. AmeriCare representatives thoroughly explained their services. We said we wanted home care until the care needed required exceeded our capabilities. By the time we got home, AmeriCare was at the house with my dad's hospital bed and other supplies. I was impressed at their level of sincere care and professional services. This home set up would be short-lived. Four days later would be the last day he would step foot at home.

September 3, 2012, was a long day. The nurse came that morning, checked his vitals and, while his vitals seemed fine, he was more confused, slower with his words and, at times, needed two people to help him walk. He vacillated between restlessness and no activity. Between around 9:30 am and around 4:00 pm, his skin color changed dramatically; his pallor was yellowish. His breathing seemed shallow, he coughed, and he seemed cold, yet perspiration covered his body. His blood sugar was stable. I made him a sandwich and he ate only a fourth of it. This was all he had to eat this day. He wasn't hungry. I even teased him, saying I could get chocolate ice cream. He looked up at me as if I were speaking a foreign language. As he looked up at me from the living room recliner, his eyes were half open and they had a glossy, teary look. This was a look I hadn't seen since minutes before my mom passed. Steven and I got him to his room and helped him lay down around 3:00 pm. I immediately called his nurse, reporting his changing condition and asked that he visit again.

I checked on him around 3:30 pm with no change. Around 4:00 pm, Amanda checked on him. She saw blood spurts coming from his mouth to his face, bed sheets, and the surrounding area. He was nonresponsive. She moved him to his side and yelled for me to come now. When I saw him, I felt he was likely going to die within a day or two. I was behind him, keeping him on his side while Amanda was in front of him wiping his mouth. Soon hospice transport arrived and took us to their inpatient facility, "The Villas." Before transport arrived, we had at least two more bouts of seizures with more blood. At one point, his face, hands, and feet turned blue. Then his body turned blue. Then he had another seizure. The kids assembled in his room, saying a few last words and crying. Felicity soon arrived and she was beside herself. She lay next to him, stroking his face, crying, hyperventilating, and telling him it was okay. She told him she loved him and he reached his hand up to her cheek for a moment. Then, she cried harder because she knew he heard her and this was his way of saying he loved her, too.

I accompanied my dad to hospice but not before calling his brother and advising him that the end was here. If he wanted to see his brother alive, he needed to come now. Right now. He asked how bad it was. I affirmed this time was different. This was it. It was time. I asked him to call his sister, Tandy, for me, as transport arrived. He was on the next flight to Phoenix. He arrived mid afternoon September 4 and immediately visited his brother. One look and he knew his brother was ready to go.

Felicity spent the entire day with him on the fourth and most of the day on the fifth. She and our Uncle Riley went to dinner the night of the fifth. His condition remained unchanged and they were hungry. I had this ache in my heart around 9:00 pm and had this feeling I couldn't shake. Around 9:45 pm, when Felicity came to the house to spend the night after an extremely exhausting day, I called and talked to his hospice nurse and she said his condition remained the same and I was welcome to visit anytime during the night. She asked when I might be there and I told her between 10:15 and 10:30 pm. As I stopped at the freeway exit, I received a call and suddenly my head started swirling and I became nauseous.

It was his nurse calling. She asked me how far away I was. I told her I would be there in about five minutes. She said to hurry, as my dad was active. I thought a miracle was happening. "He's active?" I said with a raised tone of voice. "Is he conscious?" She replied, "No, not that kind of active. He's actively dying." "What? Seriously?" I felt so stupid for not knowing what she meant in the first place. I had just never heard the word "active" used in that way before. She said she was going to unlock the back door and for me to come right in. She sweetly said that she needed to be with my dad so that someone was with him. I recall his respirations' being about three to four beats a minute. I called Felicity but there was no way she would have made it there in time.

At 10:30 pm, I swirled into the empty, damp, dark parking lot. I ran into the building, down the hall, into his room, dropped my purse, and slid next to his bedside like I was sliding into third base. His bedside was lowered at the ground and the nurse and I gently switched hands. She said he would go any minute. As I held his hand and stroked his face, I told him how much I loved him and everything would be all right. I felt the urge to play "Amazing Grace" by Cecilia. I love her version of this song. I put the iPad next to his ear. The music didn't stop me from hearing his rattling sounds. I felt so helpless on the one hand as it seemed he was struggling for air, like a fish out of water. On the other hand, he looked more peaceful than I have ever seen him look. He was at peace. He was ready to put both feet in and return home. I was given the gift of spending his last six minutes of life with him. He was with someone he loved and who loved him. If he couldn't die at home, I was glad that, at least, someone in the family was with him.

Time of death: 10:36 pm. With my dad, I reacted the opposite of my mom's death. I was shaken and sad with some tears but I felt relief. In fact, I felt as if 500 pounds were lifted from my shoulders. I called Felicity and let her know. I called the kids and let them know. I called Uncle Riley and Aunt Tandy. My Aunt thanked me for everything we did for him and my mom. I signed some papers and returned home. On the way home, I tried keeping myself busy by calling people. First, I called my spiritual mentor, Tarra, as we had been discussing my dad's impending death. Then, I called Felicity and the kids. At such a late hour, I ran out of people to call and simply took deep breaths as I drove home. The road never seemed so dark and long. Then, I started crying. I held on tightly to the steering wheel as if to direct all my emotions through my hands. Realizing my knuckles hurt and my arms were stiff, I took more deep breaths and resumed crying; continually wiping the tears from my face. When I parked in our driveway, I looked up and said, "I love you, dad" and silently prayed he was in peace, love and light. I was so relieved yet felt like the rug had been pulled out from under me. My last parent. Gone. The people that brought me into the world were no longer here. I felt all alone. I felt lost, sad, overwhelmed, relieved, grateful and full of love all at the same time.

Once again, I asked my dear friend, Mark, to preside over my dad's memorial. It warmed my heart to see so many of my dad's cousins at his funeral. People he worked with in the USAF and US Airways also came, as well as Aunt Tandy and my cousins in both Tandy's and Riley's families. We were fortunate to have a military ceremony and a 21-gun salute. When I was presented the flag, I held onto this for dear life as I shared it with Felicity. When I was presented the gun shells, I was caught off guard and started bawling. I screamed into Felicity's sweater on her shoulder for a few minutes so as to 'quietly' grieve. After the memorial service, we hosted dinner at a Mexican restaurant overlooking water. It was an uplifting evening. Amanda coordinated the whole thing and was a wonderful hostess. I received countless compliments about her smile; responsiveness, care, and helping people feel at home. Many who didn't already know Amanda said, "Wow, Tandy, Amanda's a mini you." I took that as a huge compliment.

Uncle Riley stayed with us for two weeks. I was so grateful he was here. He remained in Arizona with us through the funeral. He was an immense help in making calls, taking things here and there, making me yummy omelets, and taking care of clearing the 'stuff' in his room. He made it so that I could go through things in an orderly fashion. I didn't want him to leave. I felt like he was the only other male link to my dad. I felt as if I would now look to him for guidance and I knew he loved us so very, very much. I know that if I called and asked him to come, he would be here in an instant.

Still, I couldn't shake the feeling that my dad was leaving all over again. People ask me how I got through this tumultuous time in my life. My faith, my values, and beliefs about everything surrounding life, death, family, and unconditional love were key. My foundation of gratitude was critical through this experience and, of course, a family support system was one of the biggest factors. These were all things playing a role in getting through this trauma, drama, and any other 'ama' you can think of. I had strength to carry me through the good days and the bad. I had courage to do the right things for the right reasons. We all gave and received unconditional love, which carried us through. Courage, Faith, Gratitude, Love and Strength—pretty good recipe if you ask me.

CHAPTER FOURTEEN
Acceptance, Peace, and Love

"God, Grant me the Serenity to Accept the Things I Can Not Change; the Courage to Change the Things I can; and the Wisdom to Know the Difference."

~ The Serenity Prayer

Acceptance, peace, and love…it doesn't just happen overnight after such traumatic experiences and life-changing events. My dad talked a lot about death and dying. One such instance remains clear as day for me. During his initial stay in the hospital December 2009, he was unconscious and unresponsive (except to the painful sternum rub) for over a week. In between his somewhat lucid times, he told me about how he was talking with his dad. Knowing his dad passed away, I asked what they talked about. He said he enjoyed their conversation and that his dad was on the other side of the bridge. I thought that was odd and made a mental note and asked for a sign about the meaning of this. Later that evening, I was watching a TV show featuring mediums and they said that sometimes loved ones will appear to us as if we were on a bridge and they are on one side of the bridge. This is when we are on the 'fence' so to speak about whether it's our time to go. Later that same day, I happened to tune into a show when two people were talking about a dream they had where their dead loved one was talking to them on a bridge. That was certainly confirmation enough for me that he indeed was talking with loved ones who had passed.

I felt in my heart that God would not allow my dad to be spared only to leave him with such limited capacity. As time went on, my thinking shifted to perhaps this is exactly what was intended and my dad was our master teacher. What if he were meant to go through this to sacrifice for the sake of the family learning? Who knows? It really didn't matter why and I had to let go of wanting to figure it out.

"Peace is its own reward." ~ *Mohandas Gandhi*

I learned to really embrace and fully recognize whatever I was feeling. Everything we feel is completely normal and part of the process. Anger, sadness, powerlessness, helplessness, grief, depression, relief, regret, exhaustion, guilt, overwhelming feelings, irritability and the list goes on…I gave thanks for it all as it helped me to simply sit with these feelings as they came, welcome them, and do my best to stop wanting to change or control the situation. This takes practice and a very conscious effort. I found that welcoming my feelings rather than pushing them away helped the 'bad' feelings dissipate sooner.

Through all our experiences and daily conflicting emotions, our family's love for each other grew. Things that used to annoy me about my parents suddenly didn't matter. I started practicing the very wise saying and way of life, "Don't sweat the small stuff." My hope and prayer is that whether you have been a caregiver, are in the midst of going through difficult times now, or whether you are preparing now in anticipation of care giving that you learn from my experiences and take inspired action.

"Be content with what you have; rejoice in the way things are. When you realize there is nothing lacking, the whole world belongs to you."

~ Lao Tzu

Be open and transparent about your feelings. Leave nothing unsaid. There is nothing more peaceful than knowing that at the time of an accident or illness, you have communicated how you feel. What a gift for both you and your loved one. In addition to countless talks in person, I felt guided to write my dad a letter. When I started writing this letter, everything just came pouring out of me. As personal as this letter is and having intended for this to remain between us, I feel guided to include this letter here as a tribute to my dad.

"Our death is not an end if we can live on in our children and the younger generation. For they are us, our bodies are only wilted leaves on the tree of life."

~ Albert Einstein

December 26, 2010

Dear Dad:

I wanted to take time and let you know in writing all the things I've shared with you over the last year, most of it while you were in the hospital...and most of it while you were sleeping or unconscious. While I know your subconscious heard me and remembers everything, I wanted you to know these things and know how grateful I am for you.

Although the December 22, 2009 accident started our family on a journey we didn't ask for, it has given us precious time together. You have helped us all realize how precious life is and how quickly a loved one can be taken from us—when really nobody belongs to 'us'...we all belong to God and we are all here in our temporary home until it's time to graduate...to return home to God...smarter, wiser, and ideally—having lived a life we can be proud of.

I hope you are proud of your life thus far, Dad, because I am so very proud of you. Although there are things we would have done differently, that's part of life, right? Learning lessons...learning from our 'mistakes'...learning from every experience. You served our country for twenty years in the USAF, you have been married over forty-three years, and you had two beautiful daughters who turned out well. As you've often said, you were never called when Felice or I were kids to pick us up at the police station when we were growing up. You've never had to deal with partying or getting in major trouble with us. Okay, so there were the occasional minor issues, but all is well that ends well, right?

We both grew up to be strong, independent, intelligent, capable, and loving women. Me with my four beautiful kids—if you count Berlin and Felicity really starting to come into her own now. I know I'm proud of Felice for not settling—for not marrying as young as I did. I know one day soon she will find her divine male complement and have at least two beautiful kids...just like her☺ HAHA

You believe in and have instilled in me a love for lifelong learning. I was so proud of you when you attended University of Phoenix (UOPX) and earned your MBA degree. I remember when I asked you why you wanted your degree from UOPX and you said...because I want my transcript with my daughter's name on it! As your daughter and as Registrar at the time, I was so proud of you. I was proud of you because you wanted to earn your master's degree after having several careers and because you wanted to set an example for us. I am proud of you for pursuing several doctorate degree programs. My love of learning and books definitely runs in my blood and I owe that to you.

I remember us moving around when I was growing up and, at the time, I didn't like it one bit. However, in reflection, I am the person I am today because of the strength and courage to handle the myriad situations that presented themselves to me. Remember the walk I did between two gangs in middle school? THAT was hilarious.

I am so lucky to have had the incredible experiences I did in Job's Daughters. Thank you for being a Master Mason and affording me the opportunities I had growing up and have today because of this quality organization. I learned so much and I'm thankful I was able to serve as Honored Queen in CA. Thank you for being there with me, for serving as Associate Bethel Guardian (ABG) for Bethel No 19 when I first started in Jobies, for driving me all over the various states for Jobies events. Thank you for your support of everything I wanted to do from Jobies to piano to gymnastics, ballet, tap and brownies.

I remember you being there for the important things growing up. You were there for piano recitals, gymnastics classes, everything Jobies and mom handled—the Brownie, Girl Scout days, piano lessons, and Jobies. I remember and cherish our daddy walks where you would patiently answer my "Daddy Daddy, why is the sky blue?" questions.

I loved seeing you in uniform. I was so proud. I always knew that no matter what, you would protect me, you would be there for me, and you would love me unconditionally. I have always been a daddy's girl and absolutely adored you and looked up to you.... I still do...even with your confabulation☺ There have been so many memories I have of you. I will always keep these positive memories of you and will remember you this way.

I am thankful for the time we've had this year despite the circumstances. I have seen and learned so much this year. You've shared things with me that have allowed me to see you as a man…not just my dad. Answering questions in the legacy book allowed me to see you in a different light.

I love that you now freely say "I love you" to us. I think you have opened up a lot since the accident. I appreciate you for the amazing and loving father you have been and THANK YOU so much for everything including the many sacrifices you have made to ensure we had a good upbringing. My fondest memories of you are when we were together such as you teaching me the distance between mile markers, walking, helping you at work while you were in the USAF, being together at Jobies, etc.…

I remember earning the top ritual award when I was at Bethel 19. I remember when you were asked to bring the recipient of the award to the East and your face was beaming when you came to the anti room door and put your arm ready. I remember thinking, *what, I earned this award!?!* I knew you were so proud of me and I was proud of myself. I was proud of my ritual work and earning that award was one of the highlights of my Jobie career. I'm glad you were there with me and for me.

Hearing the many stories about your upbringing and the significant challenges you faced growing up makes me all that more grateful that you raised me the way you did. I know that took courage and deliberate intent on your part. You are my hero☺ One day when you were in the neuro rehab unit at St. Joe's (your first stint there in January 2010), I was filling out paperwork about your life for your therapists. Many questions were about significant events in your life. I remember asking you what the most significant thing was that you remember about my childhood. You said that you remember disappointing me. I was both surprised and saddened you felt that way because I would never characterize my childhood as disappointing— not at all. You quickly fell asleep and when you woke up you didn't remember saying that. No surprise there.

Yes, I was mad about moving the second semester of my senior year in high school. That was huge for me. I absolutely hated it. Yes, I hated having to give Pie Pie away. I hated moving away from my boyfriend at the time. That aside, I felt I had a good childhood. I had what I needed. I forgive you for anything you felt you have done to disappoint me.

When we moved to AZ from CA, I remember you hugging me as I was crying after saying goodbye when my boyfriend left our apartment the last day before we moved and you said "If it were true love, it would grow stronger. Absence makes the heart grow fonder. It will be okay. You can write, talk, and visit." I love and appreciate you for accepting my decisions and for always supporting me, even if you didn't agree or thought it was the wrong decision. In the case of my then boyfriend and later husband (and ex husband), we had Amanda, Sarah, and Steven and while our marriage didn't last, I am thankful for our children and every experience we had, even the bad ones. When I needed you and Mom the most, I didn't have to ask for help—I didn't say a thing—you both were there. Perhaps it was parental instincts or just protective mode. You doing what you did saved my life.

I knew with many moments growing up and as an adult that daddy's really don't like seeing their baby girls' cry and would do anything to make it better. I know you would have moved heaven and earth for me to be happy. I also knew you did what you had to do to make a living and provide for our family.

I love you for believing in me and for telling me I could be and do anything I wanted to. I love you for sharing with me all charts about the rule of 72, investing numbers and always giving me the resources I even remotely alluded to wanting to know about. I ask a question about stock technical analysis and boom, I would have three books on it. I ask about law and boom, I have a law book.

I am sorry for all the stupid things I did growing up, especially running away. As a parent, I can't even imagine if one of my kids were missing. I am so incredibly sorry I put you through that. I was selfish, young, stupid, and clearly thinking with $1/10^{th}$ of a brain cell. Losing a child is the worst possible thing that can happen to someone. I am so incredibly sorry for putting you through that. I'm sorry for tripping Felicity when she was little. It was just too fun seeing her trip and fall and the opportunity was there. I am so sorry for dropping Felice when she was three months old. At least I never did that again. That's more than I can say for a certain someone.... Yeah, there were things I did that were an inappropriate response to situations. Overall, I was a good kid☺ I never smoked. I never drank. I never partied. I did okay in school. I never did drugs.

I know this year has been especially trying for you on every level. Your entire world changed in an instant. Most details you know today were things we told you about what happened. You are not a burden, Dad. Mom is not a burden either. It has been my honor to serve you over the last year and take care of you and Mom. I know you feel that I have taken on the responsibilities you felt you had with Mom in providing for her. Perhaps a part of you feels like you want to hang on because you don't want to leave me with the responsibility of taking care of everything. I want you to know that when the time comes for you to return home to God, I will be at peace knowing you aren't suffering anymore and I will continue taking care of Mom. She will be fine. Felicity will be fine. It is okay to go, Dad. The trust is in order and all is well.

I know a part of you must be scared—scared of the unknown or of what will come of things. I know beyond a shadow of a doubt when the time comes for you to return home to God, you will be able to be with us and help us in ways you can't now. Should I leave this world before you do, I will certainly do the same for you☺ I feel and believe your help from the 'other side' will help us every single day until we meet again—in Heaven. I feel our relationship will get stronger and stronger as you will only be a thought away and you'll be able to help and impact our lives for the better. I am at peace.

You can be like our guardian angel. Remember the movie we saw recently, *Hereafter*, where the older brother who died saved the life of his younger brother by blowing his hat off, preventing him from getting on the train that subsequently blew up? He was his brother's guardian angel, watching over him and helping to keep him safe. Remember when I was in the hospital for my pulmonary embolisms right after Grandma Dittrich's funeral? SHE was my guardian angel then and had it not been for her and the angels forcing me to pay attention and get to the hospital, I wouldn't be here today. I'm good at identifying signs☺

The things you have said throughout this entire year lead me to believe you vacillate between the various stages of death. I know it is hard letting go—particularly of the unknown. You may not consciously know you are going back and forth. Yes, I got my self-confidence from you, thank you very much! I would not have changed any part of my childhood. Not a thing.

When you do 'graduate', you will be all knowing (I know I know, it's hard to believe you don't know everything already, huh) and you will say, "Well, all be damned, she knew what she was talking about!" I believe that death is really life everlasting. In death, we are born to eternal life. No nagging. No frustrations. No anger. No confabulating. No limiting arm or brain functions. No forgetfulness. No noisy grandchildren. No annoying dogs licking you incessantly. No waiting for anything. No pain. No limits on anything. Only love, peace, light, and joy…and the freedom to do what you want—when you want; can you say chocolate ice cream or having all the answers☺

Whether you decide your time to go is in a day, a week, a month, a year, ten years, twenty years or more, know that I am the amazing woman I am today because of you and Mom. I'm everything I am because you loved me. My beliefs and values were from you. I am thankful you are my dad. I am blessed and I want you to know it is okay to go and when you are ready, I will be there to celebrate your life, take care of Mom and Felice, talk to you every day, and I will feel safe knowing you are watching over us. I am proud of you, Dad. I am very, very proud to be your sunshine.

I love you
I trust you
I respect you
I admire you
I believe in you
I am thankful for you
I am thankful for everything you have taught me
I am thankful for the opportunity to care for you this year
I am thankful for the example you set for me growing up
I am thankful for you taking care of Mom all these years and showing me what taking responsibility is all about
I am thankful for you warming up to Roxy and Colonel (most days)
I am thankful for you keeping us safe and ALWAYS putting us first
I am thankful for you encouraging all my interests
I am thankful for the absolutely amazing father you are
I am thankful God put us together in this life
I am thankful for everything I have learned from you
I am thankful.

> *"People spend a lifetime searching for happiness; looking for peace. They chase idle dreams, addictions, religions, even other people, hoping to fill the emptiness that plagues them. The irony is the only place they ever needed to search was within."*
>
> *~ Romana L. Anderson*

Love is profound. Unconditional love has a positive impact on healing. I learned of the sacrifice, trials, and tribulations my parents endured raising me and how their childhood impacted their parenting style. When I learned why my parents rarely said "I love you" or showed affection, I felt their vulnerability and my heart opened more. What a priceless gift: an open heart, acceptance, peace, and love.

All aspects of my care giving journey were needed to gain a full perspective on this immense responsibility. This was an ***on the job training*** experience. My parents had tremendous courage. To be courageous means, among other things, to be vulnerable. We were all willing to put our hearts out there and learn from each other. Through the power of stories, everything became clear to me and it was as if leaves were falling off of a tree; no longer needed and free to reinvent itself. Here are some key lessons and an action guide to consider as we close:

1. Remember that words have power. Use them wisely.

2. Release that which no longer serves you. Holding onto anger, bitterness, judgments and other negative feelings only serve to hold you back. Release it and make peace with it.

3. Say what you need to say. You have a voice. Use it and use it wisely. Your needs are just as important as everyone else's needs.

4. Remember that this too shall pass. You may have conflicting emotions from compassion to anger and everything in between; sometimes daily. This is normal. What you are feeling is normal. You are not alone.

5. If something happened to you or a loved one unexpectedly, would you feel confident that everything is prepared and you would be taken care of consistent with your wishes?

6. Consider how you are spending each day gifted to you. How have you prepared for your last day? Are you prepared? Is your family prepared? If you died today, would you be calm knowing everything was taken care of. Imagine attending your

funeral and listening to the remarks. Would these remarks reflect your life and the legacy you hope to leave?

Take a moment and think about the top five things you've learned from this book.

What one thing could you do today that would make a positive impact on your life?

Chaos can happen in many forms. Healing can happen through many forms. Care giving can take many forms. My prayer and hope for you is that your healing is always swift and any chaos is minimal. Whether you are a caregiver today, think you might be one in the future or you think you may need care one day, may this book bring you peace, compassion, hope, and healing. May it be a valuable resource for many years to come.

Acronyms

Here is a list of terms and their acronyms found in this book or terms you may come across as a caregiver:

(ADL) Activities of Daily Living

(CHF) Congestive Heart Failure

(CICU) Critical Intensive Care Unit

(CNA) Certified Nursing Assistant

(COPD) Chronic Obstructive Pulmonary Disorder

(CPAP) Continuous Positive Airway Pressure

(CT) Computed Tomography (pronounced catscan)

(DNR) Do Not Resuscitate

(DO) Doctor of Osteopathic Medicine

(DMPA) Durable Medical Power of Attorney

(EMT) Emergency Medical Technician

(ER) Emergency Room

(FML) Family Medical Leave

(ICU) Intensive Care Unit

(IV) Intravenous

(LPN) License Practical Nurse

(LTC) Long Term Care

(MA) Medical Assistant

(MD) Medical Doctor

(MPA) Medical Power of Attorney

(MRI) Magnetic resonance imaging

(OT) Occupational Therapy

(OTC) Over the Counter medicines; i.e. multi vitamin, iron

(PA) Physician's Assistant

(POA) Power of Attorney

(PT) Physical Therapy

(Rehab) Rehabilitation

(Rehab Facility) Rehabilitation Facility

(R. Ph) Registered Pharmacist

(RN) Registered Nurse

(RX) Prescription

(SNF) Skilled Nursing Facility

(STC) Short Term Care

(TBI) Traumatic Brain Injury

(TFT) Thought Field Therapy

(TIA) Transient Ischemic Attack (mini-stroke)

(TDY) Temporary Duty Yonder/Assignment

Glossary of Terms

Acute (rehabilitation): Inpatient facility providing tools to regain skills lost due to injury and to adapt to permanent disability. Acute rehabilitation involves daily therapy; generally three or more hours a day.

Affirmations: Declaring a statement as being true and typically said in present tense.

Confabulation: A memory disturbance, wherein pockets of recollection are distorted or misinterpreted memories about oneself or the world that they believe to be true.

Craniotomy: An operation in which a bone flap is temporarily removed from the skull to access the brain. Craniotomies are often a critical operation performed on patients suffering from brain lesions or traumatic brain injury (TBI).

Essential Oils: Concentrated oil containing aromatic compounds from a plant. These scents are in flowers and leaves and are thought to have therapeutic properties. Essential oils are used in aromatherapy, massage therapy and in other alternative therapies.

Feng shui: A 3,000 year old ancient art and science that reveals how to balance the energies of any given space to assure all things positive.

Guided Imagery/Visualization: A system used for deep relaxation and well-being.

Holographic Repatterning: A therapeutic alternative healing modality in which inconsistent patterns in the body-mind energetic fields are identified and repaired.

Hospice: Care focusing on the palliative care of a seriously or terminally ill patient's pain and symptoms, and attending to their emotional and spiritual needs.

In-Home (In home health care): Home health care may include occupational and physical therapy, speech therapy, and skilled nursing. It can also involve helping with activities of daily living such as bathing, dressing, and eating.

Hypnosis/Hypnotherapy: A trance-like state in which you have heightened focus and concentration.

(Jobies) Job's Daughters International: Job's Daughters International™ is a *premier* organization for young women that provide a wholesome environment based on the foundation of high morals, love of country, love of family and friends and respect for others throughout the world.

Picc Line: A peripherally inserted central catheter. It is long, slender, small, flexible tube that is inserted into a peripheral vein, typically in the upper arm, and advanced until the catheter tip stops in a large vein in the chest near the heart to get intravenous access.

Meditation: An extended period of time where one focuses their attention on one thing.

Prayer cloth: Prayer cloths can be found in the Bible and throughout history. They were used to represent God's Divine healing power through prayer. It provides a point of contact for the release of your faith.

Psycho Neurologist: An aspect of psychology that deals with the relationship between the nervous system, especially the brain, and cerebral or mental functions such as language, memory, and perception.

Reiki: Reiki is a form of therapy that uses simple hands-on, no-touch, and visualization techniques, to improve the flow of life energy in a person. Reiki (pronounced *ray-key*) means "universal life energy" in Japanese.

Seizure: A transient symptom of abnormal excessive activity in the brain.

Shunt: A device with a hole or passage allowing fluid to move from one part of the body to another.

Stroke: The rapid loss of brain function due to disturbance in the blood supply to the brain.

Sub acute (rehabilitation): Inpatient facility providing tools to regain skills lost due to injury and to adapt to permanent disability. Involves daily therapy; generally less than two hours a day.

Thought Field Therapy (TFT): Alternative healing modality involving finger tapping in specific sequences to release or disassociation pain from an event; thus, promote healing.

Tuning Forks: Instruments producing sound waves that bring the body in balance.

Chronology of Events for Stevens-Elisala Family Between November 2009 – September 2012

November 16, 2009 – Tandy had abdominal surgery. On Family Medical Leave from work. Weight lift/push/pull restrictions for six (6) weeks.

November 2009 – Felicity was in car accident resulting in dislocated hip, broken foot, broken ribs, collapsed lung and broken ankle.

November 2009 – Mom was diagnosed with breast cancer.

December 22, 2009 – The phone call that forever changed our lives. Dad was involved in massive 21+ multi-vehicle accident on the I-10 freeway in Casa Grande, Arizona, involving multiple semi trucks and cars. Dad was airlifted to Maricopa County Medical Center.

December 23, 2009 – January 16, 2010 – Dad at Barrow Neurological Institute at St. Joseph's Hospital and Barrow's Neurological Rehabilitation center. Multiple surgeries, physical therapy, occupational therapy and speech therapy. Moved mom into home; rearranged rooms.

December 29, 2009 – January 15, 2010 – Led efforts to eliminate two storage rooms and one home full of parents' 'stuff' in between POA duties, home responsibilities, and being there for my dad. Two storage rooms (and associated monthly charges) eliminated! Things were donated, tossed, or moved to Arizona City home where Felicity resided.

January 19, 2010 – Mom had right breast cancer lumpectomy surgery.

January 20, 2010 - January 30, 2010 – Mom had intense radiation treatments twice daily (AM and PM). Medically advised she should have chemotherapy yet her overall poor health prevents this treatment option.

January 31, 2010 – Felicity involved in 2nd car accident and charged with DUI for prescription medication. Beginning of our legal battles, her health battles; including our realization she had an addiction problem.

January 2010 – Amanda withdrew from college to help family.

Early February, 2010 – Tandy returns to work.

Mid February, 2010 – Dad returns to St. Joseph's Hospital via ambulance transfer from Chandler Regional Hospital ER for subdural hematoma (brain bleed).

Later the same day – We took in Berlin who needed a place to stay.

End of February 2010 - Dad released from hospital.

Spring 2010 – Felicity moves in with us for 30 days.

Early March 2010 – Dad returns to hospital for more brain surgery including a craniotomy, a partial craniotomy, a brain infection and beginning of seizures and TIA's (mini-strokes).

Early March 2010 – Amanda resigns from FT job to help care for grandparents.

Early March 2010 – Tandy resigns from Vice President role and leaves 21+ year career in higher education administration to provide full-time care for parents.

Mid March 2010 – Tandy became a first time property manager and landlord as she leased out second Casa Grande home.

January – March 2010 – Family continues working to clear mom and dad's primary residence in Casa Grande.

Mid March 2010 – Mom hospitalized for asthma and diabetes.

April 30, 2010 – Dad released from hospital and moved to a rehabilitation center.

May 1, 2010 – Dad taken via ambulance to local ER and transferred back to Barrows within 30 hours of arriving at rehabilitation center.

May 1, 2010 – Sarah installed as Honored Queen for Job's Daughters International, Bethel No 21, Scottdale, Arizona.

May 2010 – Mom in hospital for diabetic leg infection and kidney problems.

May 2010 – Sold parents' Texas rental property.

May 22, 2010 – Dad released from hospital.

Summer 2010 – Mom in hospital for kidney and diabetes issues.

Mid – end 2010 – Sold parents' primary home in casa grande as short sale.

August 2010 – Tandy returned to work full time.

August 2010 – Dad admitted to hospital for renewed complications.

August 2010 – Mom admitted to hospital for severe leg infection.

November 2010 – Tandy diagnosed with and had surgery for cancer a third and final time.

December 2010 – Dad admitted to hospital.

January 2011 – Mom admitted to hospital.

March 2011 – Tandy, Amanda, Steven cleared out New Hampshire storage room.

Spring 2011 – Dad in hospital.

May 2011 – Sarah graduated high school.

Summer 2011 – Dad retired from US Airways.

Summer 2011 – Sold rental property in Casa Grande.

Summer 2011 – Put cat to sleep.

Summer 2011 – Mom hospitalized for pneumonia and kidney failure.

Summer 2011 – Dad hospitalized for brain bleed.

November 2011 – Tandy had sinus surgery.

Late 2011 – Put one of moms' cats to sleep.

Early January 2012 - Met the amazing man, Tim, (and his wife, Becky) that saved Tandy's dad in his accident December 22, 2009.

Early 2012 – Tandy's position at work was eliminated.

Early 2012 – Amanda returned to work.

Mid January 2012 – Tandy had reconstructive surgery for cancer.

Late Feb 2012 – Maternal Grandfather died. This was the last grandparent to pass away.

Early March 2012 – Amanda flies to Oklahoma and helps relatives plan for grandfather's/great grandfather's funeral. Due to recovering pneumonia, Tandy needed a few extra days to heal. Five days later, Tandy flies to attend the funeral.

Mid March 2012 – Tandy, dad and (eventually) Steven go to Oklahoma to help with post funeral logistics and personal matters.

April 2012 – Tandy hospitalized for pneumonia.

April 2012 – Felicity hospitalized for pneumonia. Same week. Same hospital floor.

April 2012 – Steven had emergency appendectomy.

May 2, 2012 – Dad had gallbladder surgery.

May 2, 2012 – Mom died.

May 9, 2012 –Mom's funeral.

End of May 2012 – Steven had tonsillectomy.

July 2012 – Sarah began college.

Fall 2012 – Amanda returned to college.

September 5, 2012 – Dad died.

September 14, 2012 – Dad's funeral.

September 25, 2012 – Tandy had hysterectomy.

October 2012 – October 2013 – Family healing and adjusting to new life.

November 2013 – ***Healing Through the Chaos: Practical Care Giving*** book published!

Afterward

S ince my parents' deaths, I have had major shifts in my beliefs and thinking. I've also had fallout from my care giving years. Some highlights of our family changes include:

1. I released over 50 pounds and continue working towards restored perfect health. While I have had my share of ongoing health issues, I am moving in the right direction. Steven has released over 50 pounds and Amanda has released over 30 pounds. We are all on the same page regarding health. This has all been possible with back-to-basics lifestyle and behavior. Eat right, reduce portions, indulge in moderation and move the body. I am thrilled to report this body is cancer free and it is staying that way!

"47% of working caregivers indicate an increase in caregiving expenses has caused them to use up ALL or MOST of their savings."[14]

2. We have had significant financial challenges. I spent all my retirement funds getting our family through these difficult years while unemployed. Integrating two households into one and the extra care involved made a huge dent in my pocketbook. It is very difficult to recover from these decisions. I am still dealing with the aftermath of my parents' medical bills. Be thoughtful and prudent about the financial implications of giving care.

3. My thoughts about material things have changed dramatically. Admittedly, I realized one of the ways I dealt with stress was retail therapy. Not a good combination. Of course, that came to a halt; thus helping me realize my self-sabotaging habits over the

---

[14] Evercare Survey of the Economic Downturn and Its Impact on Family Caregiving; National Alliance for Caregiving and Evercare. March 2009

years… long before care giving. We now live a much simpler life; free from most material things and it is liberating. Letting go of the old is empowering and refreshing. With this mindset, our lives are changing for the better. What a gift for my children; although they may not see it that way all the time. It is amazing how much crap we collected and how much we paid for it at the time. It is also enlightening how much things sell for; or should I say how little things sell for. eBay and Craig's list were great buddies of mine. There is little need to pay retail for anything and almost anything is negotiable. As of October 2013, we are still managing things day by day, and for the first time in my life, I've been at risk of losing our home. I know, feel and believe everything will work out. It always does. Despite these challenges, our family continues forging ahead and, while this could have deterred me from my coaching and care giving work, I refuse to let external circumstances get in the way of my mission and vision.

4. Steven is Senior Class President; active with football, DECA, Mock Trial, Junior Achievement, and other business clubs. Amanda and Sarah are both on track with college and working full-time. All three have above 3.0 GPA's and Sarah has consistently been on the Dean's list. Yes, I am a proud "Mama."

5. My life direction and intuitive knowing is clearer than ever.

6. I felt inspired to create a proprietary family care giving training and coaching system called P.E.A.C.E. ™ which stands for:

   P = Personal preparation
   E = Evaluate care needs and options
   A = Advocacy
   C = Care tips for the caregiver
   E = Engage the plan and evoke family legacy

I am working tirelessly to make a difference in the world;
one person…one caregiver…one care receiver…
one family at a time.

I would be honored to have you join my community. Let's share together, learn together and grow together.

"Like" me on facebook at: https://www.facebook.com/successful coachingtogreatness

Join my exclusive family care giving lifeline facebook group at: https://www.facebook.com/groups/familycaregivinglifeline/

I created this family caregiving group to provide support for past, current and future family caregivers. Get care giving resources and answers…and be inspired and empowered along the way. Join us today!

Join my Center for Inspiring Greatness facebook group community for inspiration and simple tips to feed your heart, mind and soul. Join us today at: https://www.facebook.com/groups/centerforinspiringyourgreatness/

Follow me on twitter at www.twitter.com/DrTandy

Connect with me on LinkedIn at www.linkedin.com/in/Tandye

www.centerforinspiringgreatness.com
www.tandyelisala.com

Visit my website for FREE resources and updates on products and services including training groups, individual and group coaching, mastermind groups and more.

I would love hearing from you with comments, feedback or questions about *Healing Through the Chaos* or your personal care giving experience. Email me at:

tandy@tandyelisala.com

Blessings for a long and healthy life full of love, family, laughter, gratitude, humor, and peace.

Tandy Elisala
October 2013

www.ingramcontent.com/pod-product-compliance
Lightning Source LLC
LaVergne TN
LVHW011222080426
835509LV00005B/276